M000043342

Master your Life with Love

How to create the most extraordinary relationship with
yourSelf and upgrade your Life from the inside out

by Noa Lakshmi

Master your Life with Love.
Copyright © 2017 by Noa Lakshmi.
Cover photograph by Danielle Werner Photography.
All rights reserved.

No part of this book may be used or reproduced in any manner whatsoever without written permission except in the case of brief quotations
embodied in critical articles and reviews.
For information www.noalakshmi.com

First edition published in 2017.
Printed in the United States of America.

Front cover designed by Mia Regala
Interior and back cover designed by Anita Johnson

ISBN-13: 978-0-692-93052-6

In Loving Dedication

I dedicate this book to the divine orchestration of Life; for this precious miracle continues to inspire me every single day.

To all the great teachers who came before us and are still living in us; all who which dedicated their lives to spreading the light of truth.

To Mother Earth who nourishes us all without asking anything in return except for our loving stewardship; may we all treat her with gentleness, loving kindness, and reverence.

To the hearts and souls of all sentient beings; may we all live in peace with ourselves and one another.

To my incredible parents; your unwavering love and support has been one of the greatest blessings in my Life.

To all of those who played their part in bringing this book to Life; each and every one of you is an angel I'll forever be grateful for.

To all the readers who are dedicated to their personal transformation; thank you for playing your part during these pivotal times of our human storyline.

To myself; where I've come from, who I am today, and who I am becoming. May I (and all) continue to live in Love and gratitude for the rest of our lives.

Contents

Introduction

Once upon a time there was a little girl. Let's call her Noa. Little Noa always questioned the state of our planet because what she saw in the world didn't make sense to her. She couldn't understand why people didn't get along. She couldn't understand why people fought or didn't speak with one another. She couldn't understand governments, borders, and wars. She couldn't understand why people killed animals or each other. She couldn't understand why people who are in fact alive, look and behave like they're already dead; none of it made sense to her.

Except for one thing; one thing that somehow did make sense. It was a very distinct voice echoing within her, a voice that kept saying: *You got this girl. Be you and keep following your heart no matter how the world around you seems to be or act.* That same voice is still living inside of little Noa stronger and louder than ever, and even though that little girl is not so little anymore (at least not on the outside), her essence and presence are very much part of who I am today. That same voice which I've become very close and intimate with, has been my guide throughout the years, teaching me that the Life I have been given as a human being is a precious gift; a gift for me to utilize with responsibility and care.

As I continue to grow and learn from Life's never-ending display of experiences, one thing remains unchangeable and clear: Each individual human is a unique world onto itself, even though there are seven billion humans on this one planet. Our human specie is extremely diverse and the differences among humans are endless – different colors, shapes, thoughts, beliefs, languages, attitudes, needs, desires, drives, points of view, dreams, inspirations, Life choices; the list goes on and on. Some humans are happy, some are not. Some humans choose to Love their neighbor, some choose to kill them. Some humans live in complete peace while others are constantly experiencing turmoil.

Yet, it seems that we all have one thing in common no matter what. That commonality is the fact that each and every one of us has been given the gift of Life in the shape of a human being. As such, we each get to inhabit our own individual world from the moment we take our first breath until the very last. No matter how different we all seem to be, no matter which path you choose to travel personally, each and every individual is responsible for their own personal world. There is no way around this rule and it applies to all of us. Wouldn't you say this is something we can all work with? If I had known this when I was a little girl, Life would have made so much more sense. But hey, most of us need to circle the block (and the sun) a few times before getting on board with what's actually going on.

When I realized that each human is a whole universe all of its own and that we are all connected – not only to one another but to *everything* around us, the picture became much clearer. If every human being has been given their own individual world, their own personal domain let's say, a personal domain which can be designed and operated according to one's personal choices, why not learn how to master this domain? I mean, what else would I want to do with my own individual world? Why wouldn't I want to learn how to master it to the best of my ability? After all, when someone gives us a precious (and extremely sophisticated and multi-functional) gift, would we just let it sit in the basement or would we, at the very least, read the instructions and give it a try?

"Self mastery is the ability to make the most out of your physical, mental, emotional, and spiritual health. In other words, to be the best you can be."

If you're reading this book, you're most likely interested in mastering your Life or at the very least intrigued by the concept. Self-Mastery is a road one chooses to take. It is not the end goal to Life because Life is a journey. A journey to where? Who knows… but the roads we choose to take will indeed affect the quality of our journey. And since we're here at this time, experiencing Life as human beings, might as well make it a good experience! For me, being on the road of Self-Mastery means that I choose to occupy my own domain in a way that demonstrates integrity, gentleness, compassion, Love, and true well-being. On this road I choose undying dedication to loving mySelf, bettering mySelf, and fine-tuning my instrument to the best of my ability. In its essence, *Self-Mastery is the journey of becoming the master of your own domain in order to make the best out of what you have been given.*

Simple? Yes. Easy? Well, not always. But it's so worth it.

After many years of personal exploration, personal growth, spiritual practice, rich Life experiences, work with clients, and an unwavering dedication to my Life's journey, I've come to realize that Self-Mastery was my agreement with God (*and before we continue, a word about God because I know it's a touchy subject. I use the word God freely throughout the book. It is completely unrelated to any religion, religious dogma and its definition of God. God to me is Life. ALL of Life. It's the unexplainable and mysterious force that orchestrates our creation in its totality. More on that later on).* With that said, I believe that each of us on this planet has a predetermined contract, an agreement of some sort with God. The fulfillment of that agreement is not only for your own individual journey, but to also help and uplift others on their Life journey in greater service to humanity and our planet. If you feel compelled to master your Life, know that becoming the master of your own domain goes way beyond the personal arena.

Of course, Self-Mastery does lead you to a better Life. Exponentially better. It leads to supreme well-being and radiant health. It leads to sharp mental clarity and unshakable focus. It leads to emotional balance and extraordinary inner peace. It leads to fierce courage and bold confidence. It leads to inner strength and at the same time flexibility of mind. It leads to vast capacities and capabilities you didn't even know existed. It leads to immense joy that is Self-generated and is not dependant on any external sources. It leads to great balance and harmony in your Life and an unwavering knowing that you are pure spirit manifested in a human body. And that is just the tip of the iceberg.

I believe it is every person's birthright to have that quality of Life and more. Not just some, but everyone. We are *all* the chosen ones because we are all here and we all chose to be here at this time whether we remember why or not. I also believe that Self-Mastery plays an essential role in the elevation of our entire human race and the regeneration of our planet. Even though Self-Mastery contains the word Self, it is far from being selfish. This is a road you choose to take (or maybe stumble upon) because you know (or soon to find out) that your own well-being, true fulfillment, liberation, and sovereignty are the essential building blocks of our collective structures.

The world is at a very crucial tipping point and we must clean things up fast, starting with extraordinary healing, transformation, true empowerment, and radical Self-Love in our own individual lives as we work our way toward real and profound global shifts. After all, what are the building blocks of every collective structure? I.N.D.I.V.I.D.U.A.L.S. Each and every one of us is a cell in this body of Life we call Earth and so each and every cell (meaning each and every human), needs to function at its best in order to restore the balance and well-being on this planet.

In the human body, cells always strive to maintain health, balance, and well-being. If any of those conditions gets out of whack, the body, with its own innate intelligence, will do whatever it takes to restore homeostasis. The more you imprint cells with well-being the more they will strive to maintain that state and the body thrives as a result. The more you imprint them with ill-being, the greater is the struggle for the body to get back to true health and balance. At that point, the body either wins the battle or shuts down.

This is a simple microcosm – macrocosm example. The human body (as the microcosm) represents the body of Life we call Earth (as the macrocosm) where each human being acts as an individual cell. Looking at Life through this lense, we can see how many of the struggles we are facing as humanity on planet Earth are directly linked to the well-being (or ill-being) of the individual cells (individuals humans). The good news is that we can do something about it. Every human being can choose to imprint themselves with either well-being or ill-being. Each and every one of us has the ability to either become the master of their domain or a prisoner of the human condition. The more we develop the ability to master our personal domain as individuals (and learn how to do it lovingly), the more we will all thrive as the global family inhabiting planet Earth at this time.

MASTERING YOUR LIFE IN A MODERN WORLD
What is all the fuss about transcendence & enlightenment?

Mastering your Life may sound like a heavy duty task, maybe not even attainable in our modern world. Some may associate Self-Mastery with renunciation of the human experience in some way – renouncing the body, the ego, the mind, our emotions, our desires, our earthly, material pursuits, and so forth. In my view, this is not what mastering your Life is about. By all means, I'm not devaluing those who choose to remove themselves from earthly matters and the immense contribution they have to this planet. However, that's not everyone's chosen path.

There are many spiritual teachings that say we need to transcend our human experience – transcend our body, our ego, our mind, our emotions, our pain, our needs and desires. I mean, how can you master your Life if you're still dealing with all of that... Or could you?

The definition of transcendence is: *Existence or experience beyond the normal or physical level.* The interesting paradox is that the gateway to go beyond the physical is in fact the physical. Through our human experience, through experiencing all of who we are and all that Life has to offer, we are able to go **beyond** what we consider to be normal. I just don't see any other reason why we've been given a body and a human existence if it wasn't for the sheer reason of utilizing it to the fullest. The question of course is HOW we use it.

Our human experience is such a beautiful and miraculous thing. Denying it or suppressing it in any way shape or form doesn't make sense to me whatsoever. I refuse to believe that we've been given all of that (and then some) just to profusely work on getting rid of it because we are taught to believe in something called enlightenment. The definition of enlightenment is simply: *The action or state of attaining or having attained spiritual knowledge or insight.* This doesn't say anything about getting rid of your ego and your mind, nor does it say anything about dematerializing your body into golden fairy dust. Just as with so many other things, we've turned something very simple into a grandiose and out-of-reach object. I'm not saying it's an easy task but it is simple; simple doesn't mean easy, it just means – let's not complicate it.

Enlightenment to me is simply an elevated state of awareness and presence in which one is fully engaged with Life's full range of experiences while directing their personal faculties in a skillful way; a way that supports one's physical, mental, emotional, and spiritual well-being. Learning how to master your Life and live in this way is a form of enlightenment. To add to that, living in a state of Love – Love for oneSelf first and foremost and Love for Life itself – is a direct route to both enlightenment and true Self-Mastery; because **true Self-Mastery cannot exist without Love.**

We can all get glimpses of this "enlightened state" when we go to some remote island on a retreat away from everything else… But what about on a day-to-day basis? What about when the rubber meets the road? That's what I'm interested in and that's the kind of mastery I'm offering you. I'm definitely not against the idea of transcending the ego or the mind or whatever it is we want to transcend, but honestly, *if we want to transcend anything, we must master it first.*

So what does mastering your Life look like? Well, having the ability to become friends with your ego, that's mastery. Having the ability to direct your desires and impulses in an intentional, constructive way, a way that benefits your Life and the lives of others, that's mastery. Having the ability to feel the full range of your emotions without being either crashed or controlled by them, that's mastery. The ability to be at peace with your mind even when it acts like a drunk monkey who got stung by a scorpion, that's mastery. The ability to feel at home in your body and take care of it like a sacred temple, that's mastery. The ability to do all of that while living Life on planet Earth, navigating relationships, career, family and God knows what, that's mastery. Loving yourSelf *every* step of the way, that's mastery.

Mastering your Life is about fully embracing your human nature rather than denying it or pushing it aside. It's about learning how to use your human experience as a constructive and effective tool instead of a destructive one. My desire is to de-mystify the concept of Self-Mastery and make it accessible in our modern world, because it can be. This book offers you a different approach – one that has worked for me and the many people I have the pleasure of guiding and working with on a regular basis.

Wherever you are in Life, if you see yourSelf as a change agent, knowing deep in your heart that the change begins with you, and are ready, open, and willing to embody your full human potential, welcome – you've already stepped into the path of Self-Mastery, knowingly or not. You will face challenges. I know I do. This is not about becoming a saint but rather becoming the best and most loving human you can be, leading a richer Life simply by shifting your habits, your attitude, and most importantly, your relationship with yourSelf.

We can't control our external circumstances but we sure can control our choices and actions. Your actions, when loving, kind, and in harmony with yourSelf and the world around you, will transform your Life in the most magnificent ways. If we can all learn to **value** and **master** the power we hold as humans, **use it wisely** and with the **highest integrity,** we then have a real chance of elevating humanity and creating a better world.

> **"One can have no smaller or greater mastery**
> **than mastery of oneSelf."** - *Leonardo Da Vinci*

HOW TO USE THIS BOOK AND GET THE MOST OUT OF IT

Since my Life's work is dedicated to health, Self-care, and true well-being, I have heaps of tools to enhance one's Life – from physical health to our connection with God. I have extensive knowledge regarding natural medicine, alternative methods, spiritual power tools, and anything else that helps us humans elevate our time here on Earth; anything that brings our best selves to the front of the stage. Having such a rich vocabulary of 'Life enhancing tools' inspired the idea a couple of years ago to create an actual guide, an A-Z pocket book with tools to use on a regular basis in order to upgrade our lives from the inside out.

I created a list from A to Z with different guidelines, tools, and practices anyone can choose from and apply. I went through my own extensive library of knowledge while also asking other people what they have found to dramatically improve their well-being and quality of Life. I thought I would just write a simple guide and that would be it but I kept that list and put it on the back burner. Two years later, as I started writing this book, that list came back to Life and I decided to incorporate and sprinkle all these different tools throughout the book.

The quality of the relationship you have with yourSelf is the foundation to mastering your Life. Therefore, much of this book is dedicated to exploring that topic and how you can cultivate the most loving and fulfilling relationship with yourSelf on a consistent basis.

This book offers plenty of essential tools to use in your Life. Many of the sections include meditations, affirmations and other recommended activities that will help you align with your greatest potential. Some you'll find simple while others will require more time and focus. You may face strong resistance to some of the ideas and practices you are going to find here. Your experience will be unique to you and you alone, depending on your current Life circumstances, state of mind, perspectives, beliefs, physical health, and personal history. Just keep your mind open and take into your Life only that which speaks to you.

Within the different sections of the book you'll also find some serious questions and honest inquiries designed to make you dig deep into your heart and soul as your examine your Life and your relationship with your-Self. The amount of time and depth you spend in contemplation and implementation of these questions, suggestions and practices will correlate directly with the transformational power of your commitment to yourSelf and your chosen destiny.

This book isn't only going to open your mind to a new way of thinking and relating to yourSelf but is an actual guide you can use on a regular basis. I believe that actions speak much louder than words so in order for us to experience real change in our personal lives and in the world at large, we must walk the talk. The key to your success with the principles presented in this book is commitment – commitment to taking the actions you need to take and to **be kind to yourSelf every step of the way.** This takes practice. And patience. And Love.

Now let's be real. Becoming the master of your own domain doesn't mean you won't fall off the horse ever again (because you will). That's not the point. The most important thing is your commitment to becoming the best you can be and to consistently align yourSelf with the highest road for your Life. Falling off the horse is part of Life but jumping back on is what makes you a real jedi. I'm going to show you how to change your Life forever by changing your habits and the relationship you have with yourSelf. In turn, you'll be rooted in your Self-Mastery, positively impacting the world with every choice you make.

To get the most out of this book, there are a few important base-lines I would like to present right from the start:

1. ***There is no such thing as instant gratification.*** I mean, of course there is… Just not when you're committed to mastering your Life (that's part of the deal, sorry). You can't expect real results without real commitment and genuine effort. Seeking for instant gratification is one of the most destructive patterns of our modern world; so we want to step away from it. What you'll find in this book is not another "fast-food" spirituality like so many of the programs and techniques out there these days. This is a way of *being and living in the world*; not just a quick fix. The bottom line is that you'll need to develop a certain level of discipline. And if you are one of many who has a strong aversion to the word discipline, consider this:

Discipline is just choosing between what you want NOW and what you want MOST.

Enough said.

2. Right now, you need to decide that you are going to dedicate your body, mind, heart, and soul to this journey (and by journey I mean YOUR LIFE. Your *best* Life). The word 'decide' comes from the Latin verb 'decidere', which means to 'cut off'. When you decide that you are going to do something, you cut off every other possibility. That's the power of COMMITMENT. Which leads to #3...

3. Once you decide to embark on this adventure, I ask you to show up with passion. Show up with intention. Show up with devotion. Show up and mean it. YOU are the guest of honor in this party, so show up for yourSelf and treat yourSelf as such.

4. Anything that stops you from fulfilling your greatest human potential and your Life's highest purpose and distracts you from your commitment can be considered toxic. I know it sounds harsh but that's my honest truth. *Once you experience the power of this way of living in action, you won't likely ever want to go back.* I will expand on that later in the book.

5. Stay committed and consistent with the guidelines and practices offered in this book and in turn, expect to find inner peace and Life-altering transformation. Here's the deal though: *YOU MUST MAKE TIME FOR YOURSELF.* Even if that means 10 minutes a day to begin with. This is by far one of the most important building blocks of this entire journey. Without this essential piece, your foundation will be very, very weak.

6. You will be asked to dig down into the deepest places within you. You will be asked to examine your beliefs about yourSelf, about God, and about the world around you. It's in the highest alignment and synergy of those relationships that you will find profound results.

7. If you fully dedicate yourSelf to this journey, with a clear understanding that WE are the ones we've been waiting for and that you are here to create heaven on earth (rather than expecting heaven to be somewhere else we might get to one day), you will be deeply connected to the source of divine intelligence; the same intelligence that is responsible for Life itself. Most importantly, you will learn how to operate from that place on a consistent basis.

8. The more you align yourSelf with God and with your own soul, the fewer the harsh lessons and the shorter the learning curve. Living in harmony with the temple of your Life - body, mind, heart, and soul, puts you right on track with your highest purpose. Now, just imagine a world of individuals living from that place...

THIS IS THE BEGINNING OF BRINGING HEAVEN TO EARTH.

Welcome Home.

·

PART ONE

THE WAKE-UP CALLING

Chapter 1

A Love Journey into Self-Mastery

"What we are about to undertake is an expedition together, a journey of discovery into the most secret recesses of your consciousness. And for such an adventure we must travel light, we cannot burden ourselves with opinions, prejudices, conclusions that is, with all the baggage that we have collected over the past two thousand years or more. Forget everything you know about yourSelf; forget everything that you have thought about yourSelf; we are going to set up as if we know nothing." *-Krishnamurti-*

A DIFFERENT APPROACH

How many times have you felt extremely motivated to start making better choices in your Life thanks to a certain experience (or no experience in particular), only to find yourSelf facing the same challenging wall over and over again? How many times have you promised yourSelf to stop this and to quite that, to get healthier, to do more yoga, to meditate, to go to the gym, to do more of what you're passionate about, to stop being in toxic relationships, to stop talking shit about yourSelf (and other people), to get more sleep (or maybe to get out of bed), to be nicer to your mother, to stop complaining, to sing more, to dance more, to in-joy Life more, to pursue your dreams… The list goes on and on so feel free to add your own.

The point to this is not to make you feel bad about yourSelf but to simply say we all go through these cycles, each of us in our own way facing our own demons. (And please, don't let that word scare you. Soon enough you'll become very close and intimate with your demons if you're not already). God knows I've had my fair share of going through the same loop throughout my Life.

I'll tell you a little secret: I used to be my worst enemy. Really. That was one of my demons. I wanted to change everything about mySelf; from the way I looked to the way I felt on the inside. I was constantly comparing mySelf to other people and feeling I wasn't good enough, pretty enough, skinny enough, talented enough, attractive enough; the list was endless. The same determination and discipline I've been gifted with was used by me in a very destructive way where I spent many years dealing with eating disorders and extremely distorted Self esteem. Clearly, I didn't know who I was and I didn't appreciate and Love mySelf the way I now know we were all meant to experience ourselves in this Life. I was addicted to my emotional pain and my own toxic thoughts about mySelf which led me down a very dark road.

Thankfully, my healing and transformation journey began at a relatively young age when I discovered yoga for the first time. That was the catalyst for my spiritual quest, a quest that continues to evolve as I aspire to learn more about Life's greatest wisdom. One thing I've definitely learned thus far is that we each find our way back to ourselves in a uniquely designed way; our only job is to listen and follow the guidance Life gives us. That guidance can be a little tap on the shoulder or in some cases, a two-by-four right on your head…

After dedicating over a decade to my own personal development and client work, I couldn't help but wonder if there is some type of magic glue that can make our healthy choices stick? And not just for a week or a month but for good? You know, something like a cosmic super glue. What's the real shift that needs to happen in order for someone to say 'enough' and walk away, into a better Life? An elevated Life? A healthier Life? A Life of meaning and true fulfillment? (And I'm talking about deep fulfillment, the kind of fulfillment you feel deep inside regardless of any external circumstances). What is the driving force, **a Self-generated driving force** that can consistently align us with the best and highest choices for ourselves?

Ready? Here it is:

YOU MUST LOVE YOURSELF INTO SUBMISSION.

The End.

Well, it's that simple but yes, it's not really the end. This is actually only the beginning…

LOVING YOURSELF INTO SELF-MASTERY

I can't talk about mastering your Life without laying down the foundation of Self-Love first. To me, that is the ultimate and strongest foundation there is. As you're going to discover throughout this book, these two go hand in hand, like two best friends or inseparable lovers. The more you strengthen your foundation of Self-Love, the more you'll be able to expand the structure of your mastery. You'll be able to keep adding more floors to your structure but you must continue to strengthen your foundation. See this as a mountain you choose to climb but with this adventure, every time you think you've reached the most magnificent peak, Life will nudge you to keep on climbing… Because the nature of Life is ever-expanding. The nature of Life is a direct reflection of your own true nature – EVER-EX-PANDING; and oh so magnificent.

So going back to my demons, the biggest and most relentless inner demon I've been gifted with on my journey was that vicious voice within me; a voice that was always extremely dissatisfied (and that's a real understatement) with who I was. The brutal truth is that I kinda hated mySelf and didn't think I was worth much; or anything, for that matter.

After reading this, you might think that I must have had a horrible childhood or that I wasn't loved enough. Actually, my Life and upbringing couldn't have been more of the opposite. I'm the youngest of three, a baby girl after two boys. My parents were beyond elated to have a girl and with two significantly older brothers, I was the little princess of the family. To say I didn't receive Love as a child would be far, far from the truth.

I am one lucky human who was blessed with a loving family and a very protected and supported childhood. However, just like anybody else, I had my challenges growing up. My parents, as loving and wonderful as they were, weren't perfect and like most of us, I was subjected to the toxic messages of our society, left and right.

These toxic messages (which unfortunately are still very prevalent today) are the ones which condition us to believe we are not good enough and that there's something "out there" to fix our perceived imperfections. I know for me, that was a big contributor to my feelings of inadequacy and low Self-esteem, especially around body image. These toxic messages are designed to make people feel small, unworthy, incomplete, and dependent on something external.

Why am I bringing this up? Because it's important to understand that a big part of mastering your Life involves your personal healing journey. That journey is about retrieving some essential building blocks back into your Life, building blocks that may have gotten lost along the way or perhaps building blocks you never even received in early years; for which by the way, there's no one to blame. Our parents did the best they could with what they had so it's best for everyone involved to stay away from pointing any fingers (more on that later in the book).

These **essential building blocks** are extremely necessary if you wish to build and establish a solid inner world for yourSelf. This inner world of yours has a gateway and this gateway leads you to discover and experience your wondrous, miraculous, powerful beyond measure, and ever-expanding personal domain. Becoming the master of your Life is the key that unlocks this gateway. However, there's another factor to this equation. Self-Mastery is a key that comes with a combination lock and the code for that lock is L.O.V.E – the Love you must give yourSelf first (in all its various ways) for the gateway of your true masterful powers to fully open up within you. There are those who try to force their way through the gate and there are those who insist on trying different keys and combinations for a very long time, hoping one of them might fit eventually. There are also those who hope somebody else will do it for them instead of figuring it out for themselves.

Forcing our way in is probably the most common attitude in our day and age – being hard on ourselves, bullying ourselves, harshly criticising ourselves, micromanaging ourselves to the ground, comparing ourselves to others, and all the other unkind and judgmental ways we've been taught to approach ourselves. This attitude leaves us feeling small, powerless, not good enough, and unvalued. In a more goal oriented, masculine, patriarchal society like the one we've lived in for so many generations, many people have adopted this kind of approach; it has been programed into us and has become our default approach. Why "waste" your time loving yourSelf if you can just force your way in by becoming your own worst critic... This approach might crack that gateway a little bit but it won't take you very far. If you want to master your Life and truly thrive, and I'm talking about THRIVING, not just living, one of the things you'll need is *sustainability*.

If it's not sustainable for your Life, the same thing that got you in will eventually become your biggest obstacle.

(And by the way, can you see the parallels with this kind of attitude and the state of our planet)?

Self-Love is a combination code which contains different digits. Even though the code applies to all of us, every individual needs to discover and retrieve their personal digits for themselves. One of the most essential digit to this Love code is your personal journey of learning how to become your own mother and father, your own best friend, your biggest fan, biggest cheerleader, and your own loyal companion for Life. Because you see, even with all the Love I did receive as a child, I still had a big, loud demon inside my head telling me I wasn't good enough; nothing external made the damn thing go away. Don't get me wrong, the Love and support we receive from our family and friends is crucial and very helpful – however, it's our responsibility to take it from there and give that Love and support to ourselves **unconditionally**.

Relying on external sources to satisfy our basic needs for Love, acceptance, nurturing, acknowledgment, appreciation, respect, and care is a bottom-less pit. An extremely deep one. That state will keep you wanting, chasing, craving and needing forever – whether it's food, drugs, relationships, sex, work, social media, entertainment, and God knows what. You can start identifying what your thing is and how it's connected to some type of an internal void. (And nothing to be concerned about… We all have our demons, even as a master).

The idea that we can rely on external sources to fill us up is like putting a bandaid on a deep, open, blood gushing cut. And I'm being a bit dramat-ic on purpose because nobody teaches us that. There are *way* too many people walking around with big, bloody, gushing wounds on the inside, trying to cover it up with temporary fixtures that will never take care of the actual cause. On the outside they appear to be "all put together", maybe even happy, but the reality on the inside is vastly different than what meets the eye. I talk to people almost every day only to come back to the same conclusion over and over again:

Most humans are completely blind to their own innate divinity and magnificence. They live under the impression that they need to be something or prove something before they can be worthy of their own (and of others') Love and appreciation.

Ouch.

I don't know about you, but to me that sounds utterly absurd. And very painful.

To really drive this point home, I like to use this quote I found in which I added my own twist to as it relates to Self-Love and the transformational power it holds. The quote is by Wes Angelozzi: "Go and Love someone exactly as they are and then watch how quickly they transform into the greatest, truest version of themselves. **When one feels seen and appreciated in their own essence, one is instantly empowered.**"

My addition to this quote is: **THAT SOMEONE IS YOU.**

RADICAL SELF-LOVE

Let's face it, who doesn't like to feel seen and appreciated by others? Who doesn't like the feeling of being fully accepted for who they are? When have you ever felt comfortable in a relationship or an environment where you were criticised at best and completely ignored at worst? How about being in a relationship in which your partner/ friend/ parent doesn't acknowledge you or express their Love and appreciation often? And even worst, most of the time your "faults" and "fuck ups" are pointed out for you to feel guilty and ashamed about… You're starting to see the point?

How often do we give ourselves this "royal treatment"? Most of us would probably say, quite often. This is serious business my friend; a serious disease in our collective experience. There is a cure though. A very tangible and accessible one.

Fortunately enough, we can choose to walk away from situations and/or relationships in which we don't feel honored, appreciated, accepted, and loved (and if you're still struggling with this one in your Life, boy oh boy, am I glad you're reading this book!). But there's one relationship you can never bail out of, the most committed relationship you're ever going to be in; 24/7, 365. There's one place on this Earth you'll always be in no matter where you go.

You've guessed it right. That someone is YOU, and that one place is within you. This is a lifelong contract you've signed with yourSelf, so might as well make the best of it. Now, the only way (or at least the most effective way I've found) to make the best of it is by treating yourSelf as the guest of honor that you are. To see yourSelf, appreciate yourSelf, and Love yourSelf like you would want other people to. Become your most loving parent, most loving friend, and most loving partner (for some of us it might be the parent, friend, or partner we've never had).

Quite often we hear the term Self-Love, but what does Self-Love really mean? How does it feel? What does it look like on a day-to-day basis and how can it be the number one choice that will empower all other choices in your Life? How do we shift Self-Love from a concept into a way of living in dedication to yourSelf, your well-being, and the well-being of humanity and our planet?

Within the pages of this book, you'll find answers to these questions. Remember, this is not a magic pill. It does work like magic but it also requires diligence and dedication. Once you dedicate yourSelf to truly loving your-Self and to shifting your perceptions about who you are, your Life will completely transform in the most miraculous way. Things you may have been wanting to change for years will effortlessly fall away to make room for the new. That's the magic. However, you must be an active participant and know that years and years of not loving yourSelf or treating yourSelf poorly are not going to disappear overnight. I Love this quotation by Mark Twain:

"You can't throw a bad habit out the window. You have to walk it slowly down the stairs."

Shall we walk together?

WE ARE ALL LEARNING TO WALK AGAIN

As I've mentioned earlier, it is essential we learn how to become our own parents. And why is it so essential, you might wonder? Because the funny thing about becoming the master of your Life is that you first must acknowledge and nurture the innocent child within in order for the master to take over. And if you think you left that innocent child behind just because you have a savings account and a real job, think again. That little child lives inside of us from the moment we take our first breath and all the way throughout our Life's journey.

If you don't believe me, I invite you to start observing your feelings and emotions more closely next time you don't get what you want, when someone treats you poorly or when you get rejected, neglected, ridiculed or not included in something. As grown-ups, we might deal with these situations without throwing crazy tantrums (although that's not always the case) but at the end of the day, when you let your guards down and get radically honest with yourSelf – the hurt is real. So is the disappointment and the pain. All of a sudden you're back to being five again.

I don't want to turn this into a psychology book but we can explain this phenomena by simply understanding the basic structure of our ego development (and no, the ego is not the enemy). The same basic structure can help us shine more light on some of our deep internal challenges which are mostly unconscious and hidden underneath the surface. (Oh yeah, this is probably a good time to mention that Self-Mastery comes as a package deal – you must deal with your "stuff"). So entertain me for a moment as I take a slight detour into the world of psychology…

According to Sigmund Freud, human personality is complex and has more than one single component. In his famous psychoanalytic theory of personality, personality is composed of three elements – **Id, Ego, and Super-Ego.** These three elements of personality work together to create complex human behaviors. Each component adds its own unique contribution to a personality and all three elements work together to form complex human behaviors.

Let's breakdown these three elements in a very simple way:

1. **The Id:** The Id is the only component of personality that is present from birth. This aspect of personality is **entirely unconscious** and includes the **instinctive and primitive behaviors.** The Id is driven by the **pleasure principle,** which strives for immediate gratification of all desires, wants, and needs. If these needs are not satisfied immediately, the result is a state anxiety or tension. (Sound familiar??)

2. **The Ego:** The Ego is formed around the age of two. It is the component of personality that is responsible for **dealing with reality.** According to Freud, the Ego develops from the Id and ensures that the impulses of the Id can be expressed in a manner acceptable in the real

world. The Ego functions in both the conscious, preconscious, and unconscious mind.

3. **The SuperEgo:** The last component of personality to develop is the SuperEgo. According to Freud, the SuperEgo begins to emerge at around age five. The SuperEgo is the aspect of personality that holds all of our internalized moral standards and ideals that we acquire from both parents and society – **our sense of right and wrong.** The SuperEgo provides guidelines for making judgments. The SuperEgo is responsible for our feelings of pride, value, and accomplishment (when we stay within the SuperEgo parameters of good vs. bad) and our feelings of guilt, shame and remorse (when stepping out of the same parameters).

According to Freud, the key to a healthy personality is a balance between the Id, the Ego, and the SuperEgo. I'll add that achieving this balance is a must on your Self-Mastery journey. Harmonizing these three different elements creates a state of harmony within you and is felt by you as what I call a *unified field*. When this field is rooted in Love, integrity, and peace, it becomes a powerful vessel of creative Life force. In other words, that powerful vessel is what our true and full potential as human beings is all about.

This is probably as 'theoretical' as I'm going to get in this book. I do find this simple breakdown of personality very helpful in the process of learning how to become our own parent because becoming a good parent for ourselves (just as much as with our own children), requires us to understand the different elements operating within us and if (and where) there's disharmony. The art of mastering your Life is about befriending, embracing, and loving ALL of the different elements operating within you and learning how to work with them in a way that elevates your Life and the lives of others.

With this basic understanding you can see how different elements of the personality show up at different times throughout your Life. How we express each and every element and the quality of the relationship between these different elements will determine our attitudes, choices, and actions. That little innocent child within us contains all of those three elements and until we become aware of that little child and give it the right attention, it stays trapped in the unconscious alongside our instincts and primal needs; and that can be a very dangerous territory. By becoming the master of your Life you learn how to work with this little inner child and guide it in a **loving** way.

Learning to be the master of your own domain is not a forceful act. Force can only take you so far. It is not sustainable. Force doesn't bring a state of harmony nor does it create a space for you to thrive. The purpose of your mastery is to create space in your consciousness to expand, grow, and flourish. In the same way you would approach a little child who is learning to walk – with encouragement, praise and loving words – so too would you approach yourSelf and your ever-unfolding Life's journey.

Chapter 2
The child within – Getting close and intimate with your Ego

This is an extremely large topic that deserves a whole entire book of its own. What I'm looking to convey within the framework of this book as it relates to this topic is the importance of:

1. **Acknowledging** that this child still lives within you (and always will no matter what your age is). We must start with this basic premise.

2. **Accepting** that child as an integral part of who you are and therefore deserves your attention.

3. **Connecting** your wounds and shadows to that part of yourSelf and therefore approaching your Life's journey with more understanding, compassion, appreciation, and Love.

4. **Seeing** the connection between what we call 'The Ego' to your inner child and how certain patterns and habits are directly related to a ne-

glected inner child – an inner child who is desperately craving your Love and attention.

5. **Learning** how to become your own loving parent (which is even more important for those of us who didn't receive sufficient nurturing and Love growing up).

To me, Self-Mastery goes hand in hand with wholeness. It also goes hand in hand with awareness. **Acute** sense of awareness actually. *Your level of Self-Mastery is dependent on your openness and willingness to dig deep into your own unconscious in order to bring the shadows into the light*; and shadows are merely parts of ourselves we are not aware of. There's nothing wrong with them, they just need to be illuminated. To do so, we need to get ourselves a bit more educated as to how the human psyche operates.

As the master of your Life, you owe yourSelf the gift of working with ALL of your shadows and transforming them. It's the work of an alchemist and inner alchemy is necessary for your mastery. But just like any other alchemist, it's impossible to work in the dark. The first step is to turn the light switch on so you can see clearly, distinguishing which is what and how to work with it; because searching in the dark will not take you very far.

We turn the light switch on from within by first acknowledging that this little child still lives inside of us (and is demanding our attention!)

As I've discussed in chapter one, your current age and Life circumstances have nothing to do with your inner child. **Everyone** carries that part in themselves. Your awareness of it (or lack of) is what makes the difference. Let's compare it to gravity. Is gravity still going to affect you even if you don't know it exists? Would you be floating off the ground just because you've never heard about a thing called gravity? I'd say probably not.

Gravity is what we call a natural law in our physical world. But we have spiritual laws just as much as physical ones and they apply to all of us whether we are aware of them or not. The whole point of mastering your Life is to increase your level of awareness because knowledge is power; and I'm talking about Self-knowledge.

It was Socrates who said – **Know ThySelf** and by that he meant that " People make themselves appear ridiculous when they are trying to know obscure things before they know themselves." Building on to this important discovery, it was Plato who added that "Understanding 'ThySelf,' would have a greater yielded factor of understanding the nature of a human being."

The more you know about yourSelf – the more power you have to re-create yourSelf anew.

Imagine yourSelf not knowing a thing about gravity. You've never heard the word or anything about it, so every time you threw an object in the air and it dropped to the ground you got upset and puzzled by the whole thing; maybe even mad at yourSelf for doing something wrong… When we're not aware of something (whether it be gravity or any other forces operating within us), what is occurring in reality can leave us confused and frustrated.

Now, let's say someone finally explained to you – 'hey, there's this thing called gravity you know, here's how you work with it.' Wouldn't you feel an instant relief? That little piece of information instantaneously shines more light on a situation, saving you unnecessary frustration and confusion. Moreover, after you learn about it and gain more knowledge, you immediately gain more power because you have the ability to work with it instead of fighting it.

> **"It is just amazing how you can struggle with something all your Life and then one day be blessed enough to discover the secret that turns the whole world upside down and gives you what you want in an instant."** - *'The Magician Way' by William Whitecloud*

Your inner child and the way it operates within you (with or without your participation) has a direct impact on you, whether you are aware of it it or not. But what if you *did* know about it? What if you did know it existed inside of you and actually learned how to work with it? How is that going to impact your reality? I say get to know that part of yourSelf and what it needs as intimately as you can. That alone will save you years of internal anguish and struggle and will provide you with a new sense of power once you start working with it consciously and constructively.

LIGHTS ON... NOW WHAT?

When the light of your awareness is on, you can see more clearly; and that makes it a heck of alot easier to navigate and see where you're going in order to find that which you are looking for. Know that just acknowledging your own inner child and accepting the fact that he or she is still very much alive within you (especially if this is very new to you), is a big step towards establishing a strong and loving relationship with yourSelf.

The other piece to this puzzle is recognizing that this little child within us is often wounded and scared. There is a sense of innocence that comes with that inner child…

A sense of innocence that wants to be more nurtured and held, but its parents are too busy for that.

A sense of innocence that wants to feel a sense of belonging rather than feeling abandoned.

A sense of innocence that wants to feel it matters rather than feeling useless.

A sense of innocence that wants to feel beautiful, seen, heard, understood, and appreciated.

A sense of innocence that wants to fully express itself, but is being told to shut up or that it's not good enough or not behaving appropriately.

A sense of innocence that doesn't understand why it's being singled out or ridiculed.

A sense of innocence that doesn't understand how come not everyone they Love loves them back.

A sense of innocence that learns to shut down its heart because it's not safe to Love.

A sense of innocence that learns to hide its authentic expression because it's afraid it wouldn't fit in.

A sense of innocence that only cares about three things:

To Love.
To Be Loved.
To Be Free.

Please give yourSelf the time to fully take this one in…

You might even need to stop here for a while and recognize which of the above descriptions is hitting home for you. It might be one or two and it might be all of them. What is important to realize is that as children, when that innocence is still very much at the forefront of our consciousness, we are extremely sensitive to what we observe and absorb from the world around us.

As children, when our basic needs (either physical or emotional) are not met, we get wounded. Children often think it's their fault if their mother or father doesn't show them Love. They think something is terribly wrong with them if people in their close circle (whether it be parents, siblings, teachers, or peers) don't accept them for who they are. All of that leaves marks on our psyche. Emotional scars (and I'm not even talking about individuals who were subjected to abuse, trauma or super gnarly childhood situations. That's a whole other topic).

Wherever you find yourSelf on this scale, the truth is that we've all had a taste of painful experiences and as children, we didn't have the logic to explain why it was happening; we just felt it. As adults we think it's all gone, but is it really? I still have a scar on my right knee from when I was nine years old. Twenty five years later and the scar is still there... faded, yes, but still there nonetheless. Do you think our emotional scars are any different?

Our emotional scars are even more crucial and worth talking about because they're not obvious. We can't see them until we decide to turn the light switch on and shine our awareness. And why can't we see them? For most of us it's a coping mechanism – since it's too painful to feel all these things we end up looking the other way or we learn to push it down. After all, we need to survive and function in this world and many of us just

don't have the right education or are not equipped enough (emotionally, mentally, and spiritually) to deal with these scars.

The result is that all of these unresolved emotional wounds get locked in our unconscious – since they need to go somewhere – and become hidden. Now, when something is hidden for a while, when something is left in the dark, it will eventually turn dark. It can turn moldy and quite toxic. Our emotional wounds, after sitting in the dark for awhile, completely ignored and neglected, start to express themselves as our personal shadows. That's their only outlet.

For a simple breakdown:

The source of our shadows is our hidden wounds and unattended emotional scars. Check.

The source of our wounds and emotional scars goes back to what we received or didn't receive as a child and the impact it had on our innocent nature. Check.

Since it was that little child who experienced whichever disappointment, hurt, frustration, neglect, lack of Love, lack of nurturing, abandonment, ridiculed, and pain, and that little child still lives within you, why not go straight to the source and connect face to face (and heart to heart) with that innocence within? Why not give that little child all that he or she is asking for? What we see as deeply rooted patterns (often expressed as shadows), are directly connected to a part of you that is extremely tender and needs the right care.

Believe it or not, that's how we can travel through time – **healing the past in the present moment and reshaping our future by living differently here and now.**

It is vital to remember that in the same way to when you were a child, without logical capacity to understand that which had left a scar in you, your inner child in the present is **exactly** the same. *That innocence within you doesn't speak logic; it speaks Love.* It speaks gentleness. It speaks nurturing. It speaks tenderness and compassion. These are the languages we speak to a child who is hurting. These are the only languages that will sooth the pain. And once we sooth the pain, we are then free to move forward.

If you want to go running but have a nail piercing through your foot, wouldn't you first take care of that? Or would you go running with the nail stuck in there while bleeding and under tremendous pain? Seems crazy, right? Even stupid, I'd say, yet we do the exact same thing with our emotional body just because it seems to be easier to ignore an emotional wound than a physical one.

In the long run though, those emotional wounds will eventually take their toll on us either emotionally, psychologically, energetically and even physically. Very often, any emotional wounds we neglect for too long end up expressing themselves as physical ailments or symptoms; just to get our attention. Because if you don't choose to actively embrace your wounds and face your shadows with Love, your shadows will come and face you one way or another. Your choice.

Think about a little child who's trying to get your attention. The child will get loud, even obnoxious and use every trick in the book until they get your attention. The more you ignore them or try to push them away, the louder and more persistent they'll get. Give them attention and the entire episode can be handled in a few minutes. Same thing applies to your inner child and how it operates within you. It may sound silly but denying the

fact that this little child resides within you is denying a big part of who you are. Moreover, this little child is actually running the show without you knowing about it.

If mastering your Life is your journey of choice, it's imperative to understand this and most importantly to start approaching your shadows with as much Love and compassion as possible. It doesn't mean you let them stay for good; it simply means your attitude towards them (and yourSelf) shifts to an attitude of acceptance. You move from suppression to illumination. From harshness to gentleness. It's an invitation to start being a lot kinder to yourSelf and your ego because you know what's behind it.

The shadow part of our ego is nothing more than a mask our inner child wears – an attention seeking device the inner child cleverly employs in order to get its needs met; all the unmet needs from the past. The inner child might be innocent, but it sure is sophisticated… extremely sophisticated. I mean, have you ever seen a child in action (or perhaps you can remember yourSelf as one), when they really, *really* want to get something? That child would do ANYTHING to get that which they desire in the moment.

That child will make any necessary adjustments to their behaviour in order to "win the prize". The child knows to put on the right mask for the right purpose. Kids would even go as far as lying or making up false promises in order to get their way. Honesty check for a moment, have you ever done that as an adult? Just so you can get what you want? It's ok. It doesn't make you a bad person, it just comes to show how that little child is running the show behind your back; or more accurately – underneath the surface.

The child isn't doing it because it's evil; it simply doesn't know better. To a child (same as our dear ego), all that matters is that they get what they want because getting what they want equals feeling safe and loved. And we all just want to feel safe and loved, don't we? But if I don't relate to mySelf (all of mySelf, ego included) in the most intimate and loving way like I would with a child, there will never be a feeling of safety and trust within me.

That is the reason why so many seek that feeling of safety and Love from external sources. Some would even employ questionable behaviours in order to get what they so desperately need and want but refuse to give to themselves. They don't feel safe or loved from within, so they base their entire Life on the false premise that these needs can be fulfilled by other people, by shopping, food, drugs, sex, by their career, etc. Yet, **there aren't enough external vices to give you that which you can only give yourSelf.**

So is our ego really our enemy? Do we need to eliminate our egoic desires? Of course not. Nothing is your enemy. Your ego has the potential of becoming your enemy, absolutely, but so does your body. And your mind. That's totally up to you. The more you master your Life the more you will discover that your ego (same as with your body and mind) can and will become your best friend. It will become your teammate you get to collaborate with, rather than an evil competitor to silence, eliminate or destroy.

We actually deepen our wounds every time we push against a feeling or a need. Every time we devalue our ego as this horrible monster that needs to be dissolved or transcended. Since your ego in merley a cute costume (and yes, sometimes more dark than cute) your inner child wears to get your attention, every time you push against it with a complete lack of compassion, you reinforce the feelings of abandonment and isolation within you. That alone gives your inner child the same messages you've been trying to change your entire Life – there's something wrong with me, I'm not good enough, I'm not loved, I'm not accepted, I'm not worthy, and so forth.

Consciously you may know that you are worthy and loved (although, unfortunately many of us walk around believing they're not), but we're talking about what's going on underneath the surface. You wouldn't want to build your structure on a surface that has an active volcano underneath it, would you? So we need to take care of this volcano and proceed from there.

The ego has gotten an extremely bad rap just because humans have the ability to use the ego in dark, destructive ways. In a world of duality like the one we live in, everything has two sides to it (and many shades of gray as well). You have the power to choose and so my hope is that you'll start choosing more Love for yourSelf; more often than not. Now that you know that your inner child is merely hungry for your attention and uses all kinds of tricks to get it, I encourage you to be the loving and supportive parent you never had. And even if you did experience Love and support growing up, just like in my case, with all the Love I did receive as a child, I still had to learn (and still learning) how to befriend the child within and parent mySelf back to wholeness.

Learning how to parent yourSelf is merely the process of learning how to support and Love yourSelf unconditionally. In my own experience, that has been the most effective way to befriend my shadows and become more empowered. Once I stopped seeing my shadows as my enemy, everything shifted. When you turn the light on in a dark room the darkness is gone. As simple as that. It doesn't take much.

Establishing a loving relationship with your inner child will automatically get you to **start trusting yourSelf more.** This is crucial. This inner trust will increase the sense of safety within you which will eliminate the need to seek it outside of yourSelf (which by the way, is one of the most predominant challenges in so many relationships). You can be trapped in that pattern for years and go through many different relationships without seeing that what you're actually looking for is your own Love and attention. But once you catch it, once the light is on and you start caring for that little child within you, you shift the pattern. You release the demon. You transform the shadows and bring the power back into your own hands (and heart).

Implementing this concept into your Life will allow you to access so much more of your innate wisdom. Cultivating more trust, safety, and Love by honoring all of who you are will give you the confidence to follow your innate wisdom when it comes to making choices in your Life – Instead of letting that little child run the show recklessly behind your back, you'll start guiding it in a conscious way. By developing an intimate relationship with your inner child, you are in fact, going to open the floodgates of joy, Love, happiness, fulfillment, and abundance in your Life.

Does that mean you're not going to have bad days ever again? Of course you will. You will still experience sadness from time to time. You'll still experience disappointment, anger, fear, insecurity, and frustration. Shifting your relationship with your inner child doesn't take your humanness away. If anything, it make you even more human. Only a more fierce human, a masterful human because you're willing to embrace all of it. And Love all of it like a parent loves their child no matter what.

Remember that Self-Mastery asks you to work with your human nature and not against it; how to work with your ego and not against it. How to work with your wounds, shadows, and demons instead of battling against them 24/7. But we must get familiar with the operating system before we start messing with it. We want to tend to it with an attitude of Love, gentleness, and care. We're not trying to break the operating system, we're just looking to install some necessary upgrades.

Your consciousness was not meant to be a battlefield. I suggest you put down the sword and shield and turn your consciousness into a playground – it's your choice how to play and who to play with so let yourSelf play. Let yourSelf be *all* of who you are. Nurture yourSelf in ways you would nurture a child – physically, mentally, and emotionally. Become your most loving parent and most loyal ally. You deserve that kind of Love and care, not just from other people but from yourSelf first and foremost.

Put this in your tool box:

Talk to yourSelf

This is by far one of my most favorite things to do – **ON A REG-ULAR BASIS**. It may become one of your most valuable tools and something you can do at any moment throughout your day. It requires getting over the feeling of being silly (or nuts) and realize that this tool is actually very therapeutic and soothing. The kind of conversations I'm suggesting you have with yourSelf are not the harsh criticism or faults pointing you might be used to… no. We're looking to shift that. We're looking to change the narrative to a more loving one. A kinder one. A narrative that actually makes you feel heard, seen, accepted, understood, and loved by yourSelf. How does that sound?

This is going to take a few different forms – you are going to become your most loving and compassionate parent, your most encouraging cheerleader, and your biggest fan. Just think about all the things a child needs to experience in order to feel loved and supported. All the things a child needs in order to feel safe to fully be who they are. All the things a child needs to gently be guided with. Then, without changing a thing, you are going to approach and talk to yourSelf in the EXACT same way.

So here's the deal:

1. During times of internal struggle and pain, whenever you're going through something challenging (either internally or externally) and are feeling unpleasant or uncomfortable feelings, approach yourSelf as that loving and compassionate parent. **These are the times you need extra Love and support, not less.**

   It's very helpful to lean on others for that support (and I encourage you to do so) but it's important to recognize that we are looking to shift *your* internal dialog with yourSelf which is something **only you can do** – not to replace external support but to learn how to give yourSelf the Love and nurturing you are deeply needing in those crucial moments. Your inner child wants YOUR attention. Nobody else's.

   For example, if you're feeling sad or heart broken, maybe you're feeling disappointed or defeated, instead of trying to rationalize your feelings or being hard on yourSelf for feeling that, let yourSelf be with your feelings and ask yourSelf this very important question – *what would I say to a child in pain who's coming to me crying right now?* Would I tell that child to "toughen up"? Would I tell that child to get lost cause I don't have time for them right now? Who in their right mind would do that?? So why do we give ourselves this treatment? I think you deserve more than that. Don't you? Let this question always guide you: **What would be the most supportive and nurturing demonstration of Love?** It is essential to ask yourSelf these questions and then give it to yourSelf without hesitation.

Is it more rest? Do you need to take a nap? Do you just need to cry? Do you need to go for a walk? Do you need to hide under the covers for a while? Do you need to call your best friend? Do you need a big loving hug? Whatever it may be, don't push it away or distract yourSelf from your feelings and needs by reaching back to destructive patterns or by condemning yourSelf for the way you feel.

The more you are willing to go there with yourSelf and give your inner child the care it's seeking, (instead of avoiding, condemning or numbing your feelings), the quicker you'll be able to move through whatever feelings or experience is in front of you. You don't need to get stuck there, you just need to give it the appropriate attention so you can move on without causing additional wounding to that little child.

Those little, yet profound acts of kindness towards your-Self are like small deposits you're making into your personal emotional bank account. By doing that, you are taking care of your emotional wounds (the hidden and the not so hidden) which allows the healing process to happen naturally, freeing you of behavioural patterns that stem from your neglected and uninformed ego/inner child.

2. As your own loving parent, it is essential to recognize the appropriate times for some tough lovin. I'm all about gentleness and Love, yes, but Love can be fierce at times. Love can be firm. So with this approach, we are learning how to compassionately (yet firmly) guide the child within, or in other words, guide our ego. If you remember the innocence of that child, the simple fact that it doesn't know any better, you realize how futile (and quite absurd) it is to get down on yourSelf, be mad at yourSelf, be harsh with your internal dialog and so forth. It's a path that leads nowhere except to some major feelings of Self-defeat, powerlessness, lack of Self-worth, and all the way to Self-hatred. Again, these are not invited to your party. Not anymore.

When relating to your inner child, the question in front of you is: **How would I approach a three-year-old?** That doesn't mean you bend your higher wisdom to accommodate that three-year-old but it does mean you understand they just need some guidance. They need to learn a better way to do things. They need to be shown a different way.

They need to hear words of reassurance and reason rather than shame. They need to be told, 'Hey sweetie, I know you really want to eat that candy now but it's 2am and your tummy hurts' Or, 'Hey sweetie, I know you really don't want to clean your room right now but you can't even see the floor with all this mess.'

You know what I'm talking about, don't you? All those things we desire to do but also know it's not good for us in the long run. Or all those things we know will make our Life so much better yet we procrastinate and resist with all of our might. You betcha, that's your inner child trying to run the show. So instead of feeling shameful or bad about yourSelf, you pull your 'compassionate yet firm' guidance card.

You talk to yourSelf (or that part of yourSelf) in the same way you would talk to a child who needs to be informed of a better way. Often times I'll have a conversation out loud with my inner child. Not only that it's extremely entertaining but it also gives your inner child an opportunity to be heard and receive the attention it's looking for. Right now, as I'm writing this book, I'm needing to have so many conversations with that little brat… (and I'm calling it a brat in the most endearing and humorous way).

The resistance I'm faced with some days is off the charts! And we all encounter it one way or another (how many times have you had to drag yourSelf to the gym, or a yoga class, or to anything that you know will be highly beneficial or productive?) After years of leaning towards the harsher approach with mySelf, I've learned that in order to shift my state of resistance (that inner feeling of kicking and screaming) and feel more at ease, I must approach mySelf and my resistance in a compassionate way. To be firm, yet to remain in a loving conversation with mySelf and explain to my inner child why we're doing what we're doing.

Let your inner child/ego know that you two are working together; because it just wants to feel included (just like we all do). It doesn't mean you follow your inner child's instructions all the time but you **open your heart to see where that part of yourSelf is coming from.** When you do that without judging or shaming yourSelf, you'll actually be able to dismantle whatever resistance you are feeling towards something. It may take some time, but again, you are making small deposits into that Love account within you; and believe me, you will hit the jackpot at some point. All it takes is loving yourSelf like you Love or would Love your own child. Shaming or judging yourSelf will become a thing of the past.

3. **You must acknowledge your every step, ESPECIALLY what you consider to be baby steps.** You are going to become your biggest fan and supporter which means everything you do becomes a grand achievement. Why is this so important? Because more often than not, we really know how to poop on our own parade. If it's not some kind of an

earth shattering accomplishment we don't even take the time to congratulate ourselves.

Let's look at that little child again. When a child does something for the first time or when they succeed in accomplishing something (no matter how simple it may seem to you), aren't you going to praise them? Aren't you going to tell them how great they're doing? What would be a boost of confidence for them – hearing words of praise and positive reinforcement, or being told they can do better, maybe even being completely ignored? Do the latter over and over again and that child's confidence and motivation will slowly diminish alongside their Self-worth and Self-value. Eventually they wouldn't even bother trying.

Same thing applies to you. The more you embrace your inner child, the more you are able to see all the ways you have been mistreating yourSelf, unconsciously diminishing your sense of confidence and Self-worth. Since we all have a soft spot in our heart when it comes to children, connecting to your own inner child and seeing yourSelf from that perspective is by far the most effective way to develop that same compassion, kindness, understanding, and Love for yourSelf.

So from now on, start praising yourSelf. Not only for big accomplishments but for *everything*. Especially as you are embarking on this new journey – every change of attitude, every new thought, every positive shift in your destructive patterns, every new choice, all of it deserves your attention when it comes to how much praise you give yourSelf! And please, don't devalue or underestimate your progress.

One thing I like to do is reviewing my day as I lay in bed at night before falling asleep. I review all that I've done and say to mySelf how great the day was and how proud I am of my-Self. If there has been a major accomplishment or progress in any area of Life (internally and externally), I make sure to fully acknowledge and congratulate mySelf for that. If there has been something that I know can be improved, I take note of that and lovingly guide mySelf in a better direction. It does take practice and I still catch mySelf pooping on my own parade at times. It's a learning process. But once you become aware of it, you have the choice to consciously start walking in the opposite direction.

Try this one on:

Write a letter to yourSelf from your past child Self

This is an extremely therapeutic process and can be quite cathartic as well. Make sure you have the right environment to do this and give yourSelf ample time for this process. I suggest you dedicate an hour to two hours (some of you may need the course of a few days to get it all out). Either way, don't rush it and allow yourSelf to feel whatever is coming up for you.

You'll need to put yourSelf back in your child Self shoes and write from that place – express all of your feelings, fears, insecurities, disappointments, hurt, pain, dreams and aspirations. What was it that you didn't receive as a child but secretly wished for? What felt confusing? Unloving? Scary? Unfair? What did feel loving, nurturing, fulfilling, joyful and safe? What did you dream for yourSelf and this world?

Find your child voice and let him or her speak to you. If you prefer speaking over writing, you can record yourSelf and then listen to it. This can be even more profound but whichever way works best for you would be the way to go. This process requires you to completely let go of your rational mind and be one with your heart. Your logical thinking will hinder this process so I encourage you to do a short meditation prior to this process so you can get out of your head and into your heart.

As a compliment to this letter, I invite you to also write a letter from your present Self to your past child Self. In this letter you want to let your child Self know how special and loved they are. Let them know they are safe and supported. Let them know that you promise to look after them and nurture them. Let them know that their dreams are important and that they matter. Let them know all the things you weren't told as a child but you know now to be extremely valuable and reassuring. Put yourSelf in the loving shoes of being your own parent and communicate with your child Self in that way.

So yes, you are an adult in this present time, but you are also a dynamic being comprised of different elements all existing within your consciousness at the same time. The past (the version of you as a child) is living in the present moment within you. The invitation here is not to get stuck in the past but to realize you can actually live more powerfully and be at peace right here and now by uniting all parts of yourSelf. You're using a past version of yourSelf to live more in Love in the present and therefore move into an even better future.

Chapter 3

Your Total Life Upgrade Begins Here

KNOW YOUR WORTH

"Self Love requires you to be honest about your current choices and thought patterns and undertake practices that reflect Self-worth." - *Caroline Kirk*

There are many factors that shape our lives – from the inner world of our thoughts, beliefs, emotions, memories, Life experiences, attitudes and perceptions to our outer world of family dynamics, different relationships, community, career, jobs, creative projects and other pursuits. Within all these different elements, our sense of Self-worth plays a very important role when it comes to how much health, abundance, joy, Love, peace, harmony and fulfillment we allow into our lives.

When we doubt our worthiness, we limit or sabotage our efforts and undermine our well-being, health, happiness, relationships, finances, and true fulfillment. This all happens underneath the surface of course, in the underworld we call the unconscious. Have you ever wondered, for example, why some people continue to accept toxic relationships or undesirable work conditions? Perhaps you used to be that person or still are. It is the level of our Self-worth that determines what kind of choices we make or don't make.

It's important to note that no one else can give you an improved sense of Self-worth. Self-worth comes from doing what is worthy.

IT IS AN INSIDE JOB.

Your **innate worth** has nothing to do with fate or circumstance. It exists as a fact of Life, like the air we breathe. It doesn't need to be raised, revitalized, or earned. But we need to deprogram ourselves from some of the bullshit we've been handed down, which over the course of our Life has formed into strong belief systems within our consciousness.

How about we dismantle some of these false beliefs so you can fully embody your divine nature and innate worthiness? To do that and to make this topic relevant for your Life, let's start with some Self-reflection questions, evaluating where you stand on the scale of truly seeing your Self-worth. I invite you to answer "Yes," "No," or "Sometimes":

- When Life gets real good and fortunate do you think, "This can't last?"
- Do you find it easier or more natural to give than to receive? Does receiving make you feel uncomfortable or think that you must do something in return?
- Does your Life feel like a series of problems?
- Does money seem scarce or hard to come by?
- Do you find your work and your relationships unfulfilling?

- Do you work long hours and lack leisure time? Do you feel guilty taking leisure time for yourSelf? Do you have a hard time doing something just for fun?
- Do you resent or envy people who take frequent holidays?
- Do you feel driven to work more, do more, and be more than others?
- Do you overeat "comfort" food, smoke, drink alcohol daily, or use other drugs?
- Do you feel uncomfortable when you receive praise, applause, lots of attention, gifts or pleasure?
- If someone asks the cost of your services, do you price yourSelf lower than others in your field because you want to be "fair"?

If you answered "Yes" or even "Sometimes" to a number of these questions, I invite you to reflect on the choices you tend to make in your Life and find the connection between those different choices and your current reality – internally and externally. By acknowledging your responsibility and the role your choices play in your Life, you find the power to make different choices.

This process of Self-reflection is not about pointing out all of your, let's just say, less than healthy and positive choices. What's done is done and we must move on. However, being honest with ourselves and our choices is an important stepping stone on this journey if we desire to improve our relationship with ourselves and truly embody our Self-worth. Discovering your unconditional worth can help you expand fully into the world which begins with this small step: gaining deeper awareness of the underlying issues and finding the solution within yourSelf.

Some of the inquiries in this book will shine a light on your current choices – what does or doesn't reflect a sense of true Self-worth and where is there room for improvement. Keep in mind that this is a learning process for all of us so be patient with yourSelf. The journey of mastering your Life is, in essence, a journey back to yourSelf – an ongoing journey of deepening this one in a Lifetime relationship by getting to know yourSelf better and by giving yourSelf the unconditional Love your heart has always craved for.

And just like any good Love story and a long lasting partnership, it only gets better with time...

So don't rush it.
Savor every moment.
The good. The bad. The ugly. The beautiful. The miraculous.
The miracle that is you.

The fuel I suggest using to run your internal engine is of course, Love. Self-Love that leads to Self-Mastery which leads to more Self-Love which leads to you being a fine-tuned instrument who operates in this world like a true master – not avoiding the world, pushing against it, or being pulled by its strong currents, but as a beacon of light with a heart full of Love and compassion carried by a vibrant body and a clear mind. This fuel you put in your tank is the essential fuel to ensure you will consistently make the best choices for your Life.

Enhancing the quality of your Life by loving yourSelf has many different expressions as I'll be describing later on. My intention is that you'll either learn something new or perhaps reconnect to an old practice or an old passion. Whichever speaks to you the most is what you probably need the most; what your body, heart, and soul are craving and maybe have been craving for far too long. Rest assure that the spark of the relationship be-tween you and yourSelf will be re-ignited! And when you have the right fuel and the right spark, you are free to drive your shiny vehicle and in-joy the ride!

Using this book and its guidelines will slowly shift you from being 'disciplined' to being DEVOTED. I just Love this word. Say it out loud. Notice the difference in your body... I'm not saying discipline is not important, it's actually crucial but sometimes it's the tiniest shift in perception that can take us to where we want to go. So this is merely an invitation for you (especially if you have a hard time with "being disciplined"), to approach this entire adventure from an attitude of devotion. Be devoted to the gift of Life you've been given... What can be more important than that?

TRUE WELL-BEING

My idea of what *true* well-being is may differ from what is commonly seen as well-being in our society. For some, well-being simply means to be healthy. Some would say that the absence of dis-ease or illness indicates health or well-being; if I'm not sick that means I'm well. For most people being just ok is good enough. Some even train themselves to become comfortable within their own discomfort whether the discomfort is physical, emotional, mental or all of the above. The familiar discomfort becomes one's comfort zone. I refer to these various "comfort zones" we place ourselves in as cages, Self-imposed prisons. We have been conditioned to pigeonhole ourselves into such tiny holes, it is unbearable to witness sometimes.

Our human composition (which includes body, mind, heart, and soul) is nothing less than a gift. Period. To disregard this brilliant instrument you've been given by not exploring the infinite ways you can use it and by not acknowledging its innate divinity, is a straight up insult to whomever you believe is your creator. To not take care of this instrument in the best way we can, to not fine-tune it (although we have everything we need to do so), and to not produce the kind of melody we are capable of with our instrument is adding insult to injury.

If you are satisfied with just being ok, don't let me stop you. To each their own. I'm assuming though that if you're reading this book, you're probably interested in being a little bit more than just ok. If Self-Mastery calls your heart you better be sure the bar will keep on rising higher and higher as you continue to explore and experience your own magnificent capabilities. These capabilities all reside within you, within your own human domain where soul and body must live as one. To separate your soul, (which is your spiritual nature) from your body (which is your physical nature) would be like separating the engine of a car from the car itself. The engine is useless on its own. So is the car. Put the two together, and you have a running vehicle.

Your soul is the running engine of your physical vehicle.

I don't need to tell you what happens when you don't take care of your car… It goes to shit. Your human vehicle is no different. By taking care of it with regular maintenance and quality services, you get to in-joy a smooth and pleasant ride. The better the car, the better the ride. It amazes me how many people actually take better care of their car than they do with their own human vehicle. I say human vehicle and not just 'body', because true well-being encompasses all aspects of who you are: Physical body, Emotional body, Mental body, and Spiritual body (just like your car has different operating systems). Caring for all of these aspects, knowing that they all interact with each other regularly is key to cultivating true well-being.

Going into each aspect is a book in itself. Each aspect is a stand-alone topic and there are many books out there discussing the different aspects of our human vehicle and the relationship between them. For simplicity's sake, I'll break down these different elements in the most basic way:

- Physical Body – The most obvious of all. It is the house that stores all of the other elements.
- Mental Body – What we call the mind. It's the place where your thoughts, perceptions, beliefs, and logic reside. It's the place we store and process information from our internal and external reality.
- Emotional Body – This element contains imprints of the emotional aspect of your memories as well as your current emotional state. It is the bridge between your physical body and your mental body. It is also that sensitive place within you, what we refer to as feelings or emotions. Your precious heart resides within your emotional body.
- Spiritual Body – Or what I refer to as the Soul. It's the driving force in your Life. The engine. And just like the engine of a car, it sits under the hood, unseen but undeniably noticeable and needed. Without the soul, we have a lifeless vehicle.

It's important for me to say though, these different aspects cannot be separated from one another. As with your car, a malfunction in one system has the potential to affect other systems. That's why true well-being is a result of a fine tuned and highly-functioning vehicle AS A WHOLE. We can then say that:

TRUE WELL-BEING IS A STATE OF FINELY TUNED, HIGHLY FUNCTIONING AND HARMONIOUS WHOLENESS.

And that goes for you personally and for humanity at large.

Using this wholistic approach is an absolute must (and I use the word *wholistic* rather than holistic, derived from the word 'whole'). We must address all aspects of our humanness in order to attain true well-being and mastery. The most important guideline of all is to always strive to stay nourished and balanced on all levels. It takes practice and a lot of Self-Love but that's why you're here reading this book. With one loving step at a time, you'll become more and more masterful and completely upgrade your Life in every way.

INVITATION FOR YOUR LIFE ASSESSMENT
YOU are the ONE you've been waiting for...

I invite you to take your time with this part and most importantly, to be honest with yourSelf – honest regarding your current choices and patterns and which of them don't reflect a sense of Self-worth. Take note as to which of these choices and patterns don't enhance the quality of your Life and overall well-being, re-assessing what works and what doesn't, what feels like acts of Self-Love and what doesn't. No need to be hard on your-Self. Just be honest and know that you are moving in the right direction.

You can record your answers and keep them in a journal, either by hand or electronically. Looking back on the notes you have made and witnessing your progress, will reinforce your new choices and attitudes which will be very rewarding. No doubt you'll want to continue moving in that direction.

Let's start with a few general Self-inquiry questions:

- What are the patterns in my Life I wish to shift?
- What are my weaknesses I do not wish to exacerbate?
- What are my strengths I can continue to accentuate?

- What is my goal? (or as I like to ask – What is my WHY?)

After you've given yourSelf the time to ponder these inquiries and have gotten clear on each one, let's move into some real Life situations, things we all encounter throughout Life. By making these assessments, you'll start seeing the bigger picture and where you need to make some important adjustments:

1. Do you make it a priority to give your body the nurturing, rest, good nutrition, ample movement, and ample comfort it needs to the best of your ability **on a daily basis**?

2. How do you choose to spend your free time? Do you spend quality, connected time with yourSelf (or loved ones) as often as possible or do you spend much of that time watching TV or endlessly browsing the Internet?

3. Do you have a good sense as to how you're spending your emotional, mental, financial, and physical energy, and most importantly, are you aware as to whether these activities bring back joy, connection, nurturing, relaxation, peace, inspiration, Love, and creativity into your Life?

4. What is it that you have a hard time accepting about yourSelf? What parts are you wanting to deny, avoid, hide or forcefully get rid of? How fully are you aware of your shadows and wounding? Do you have a hard time accepting that about yourSelf? Do you have a hard time appreciating yourSelf *despite* of your shadows?

5. What are the qualities you do appreciate about yourSelf (inner and outer) and are you able to fully see your magnificence and compliment yourSelf without feeling guilty, arrogant, or entitled?

6. Where do you reside on the **authenticity** scale?

Where in your Life are you not being real? Not being FULLY your-Self? What feels false? Not sincere?

Do you find it challenging to speak what is true for you? To express what you truly feel, think, or desire to do?

Do you put yourSelf in uncomfortable situations, whether wearing certain clothes, being in certain environments, or hanging out with certain people just because you want to fit in or impress others?

Do you find yourSelf being concerned about what other people may think about you and therefore adjust your choices or actions just so others wouldn't get upset? Do you disregard the way you feel – maybe it's tired, overwhelmed, sensitive, etc, in order to accommodate others and their desires?

The even bigger question to ask yourSelf here is: WHY? Why are you not being true to yourSelf? What is it you're faking and what's the reason behind it? Do you fear not being popular, accepted, liked, or loved?

7. Do you seek permission or approval to be yourSelf? Do you recognize that you (as much as everyone else), deserve to take up space on this planet just as you are right now and to create the Life you Love and desire for yourSelf?

8. How often do you follow what your intuition says? Do you find your-Self living in the "logical" space of your mind most of the time, suppressing what feels right for you just because it may not make sense either to you or to other people?

9. Do you allow yourSelf to dream big without contaminating your dreams with judgments, perceived limitations about yourSelf, or lack of Self-worth? Do you believe you deserve to actualize your dreams and be TRULY fulfilled and happy?

10. Do you tend to go into a dark place when it seems like you've made a mistake or do you encourage yourSelf to move on and learn from your past experiences rather than trying to change it?

    And…. Do you in fact learn from your past experiences or do you find yourSelf rehashing the past, acting out of integrity with yourSelf and with others by repeating toxic patterns such as lying, manipulating, blaming, withholding, and pretending?

11. Do you take full responsibility for all of your experiences knowing that you hold the power of deeper Self-awareness with each experience and the ability to access your intuition when it comes to making Life choices?

12. Do you trust the path that your soul is on and therefore make a genuine effort to become a conscious co-creator of your destiny?

13. Do you live in harmony with the natural cycles of your body and Life in general? How well are you in tune with those cycles and do you honor yourSelf and your well-being according to the phase you're in?

14. How much time do you spend in nature? On the Earth and with the Earth? Do you live in harmony with the rest of the ecosystem knowing that your choices impact the whole?

These reflective questions offer you an opportunity to look at your Life from a bird's eye perspective. No judgments, criticism or any sense of right or wrong. Those are not invited to this party. This process is here to empower you and put the power back in your hands. See this as motivation and fuel to start creating the kind of Life you want to live by simply shifting how you view yourSelf, your worth, and the choices you need to make to reflect that.

Chapter 4

Self-Love in Action

YOUR MOST COMMITTED RELATIONSHIP

You know that feeling when you're in Love? You've just met someone who completely captured your heart. You think he or she is the most beautiful thing you've ever seen and you would go above and beyond to bring more happiness, Love, and joy to that person. You would do anything to see a smile on their face and you will hold them all night if need to because they're sick, or sad, or just need to be held and feel loved. That person has your undivided attention and you wouldn't let anything harm them. You are devoted to that person and to cultivating the most loving and fulfilling relationship with them...

Imagine having that kind of Love affair with yourSelf. For Life.

Most people have been in Love at least once in their Life (I hope) and know what the feeling of being in Love does to one's inner world. Everything feels different, right? All of a sudden the world around you feels and even looks different. You feel so full on the inside, so elated that you start operating as a completely different person. A new person. Has anything else changed in your Life beside the fact you're in Love? Nope, nothing else… But that's all it takes. The Beatles knew what they were talking about when they said *All you need is Love.* Because once there's Love, true and deep Love, everything else follows.

Did I fall in Love with mySelf over night? Hell no. Am I still learning how to stay in Love with mySelf? You betcha. Just as with all other relationships, the quality gets better over time and we need to actively participate in keeping the flame alive. I'm not writing this book claiming to be fully and utterly in Love with mySelf; but I definitely Love mySelf now more than ever before. And that takes commitment. Real and profound results only come from committing ourselves to something or better yet, DEVOTING ourselves to something.

On my personal journey, I found devotion through my yoga practice without knowing what devotion even meant. Something about it just kept me coming back. It was my devotion to the practice (which ultimately was devotion to mySelf), that catalyzed dramatic shifts in my Life – shifts I was consciously pursuing and even bigger and more profound shifts that my soul was pursuing on my behalf.

WE ALL START SOMEWHERE...

My first experience of yoga was Bikram style. For those of you who are not familiar with that style of yoga, you practice in a room with full-length mirrors where you are asked to look at yourSelf for the majority of this 90-minute long, heated, sweaty yoga class. Sounds lovely, doesn't it? I must mention as well since the practice is done in a heated room, most people are half naked, at least the ones who are fit and look damn good in those tiny yoga shorts.

Now, for someone who didn't like her body at all it was pure torture. Most people struggle with the heat or the yoga poses but for me, the biggest challenge was to actually look at mySelf in the mirror, (tiny shorts and all), and not despise what I was seeing.

Just to be clear, I was never overweight. Not even close. But that's the whole point. We can have the most distorted ideas and perceptions about who we are – for some of us it's body image; for some it's Self-expression; for some it's their talents (or lack of), and for many of us it's a little bit of everything. The bottom line is that we are not taught to truly celebrate and appreciate ourselves. We are not taught to acknowledge our divinity so a big part of our healing journey is learning how to do just that; how to not only like what we see in the mirror but to be able to see beyond that... To be able to see our magnificence and our beauty, our brilliance and our worthiness, our true and divine nature manifested in human form. And to then make our choices in Life based on that.

How many of us are truly awake to our divine existence? And I'm not talking about knowing you are alive because I'm assuming you do. I'm referring to your magnificence. I'm referring to your AWEmazing human existence that has nothing to do with how you look, what you've done, what you do, and who you think you are or not. I'm referring to the precious gift of Life expressing itself as YOU. Are you awake to that? To the magic that you are? Not some of the time but ALL the time?

I challenge you to announce to the universe (and to yourSelf) just how magnificent you are. Come on, go right ahead, don't be shy. SPEAK IT. You can use whichever words work for you. Just say it. It might take a while to say it and really mean it but let's just start by speaking it first:

I AM MAGNIFICENT.

I AM AMAZING.

I AM A GIFT.

I AM DIVINE.

I AM WORTHY.

How many of us have a hard time making these announcements? Raise your hand if you're one of them… How many of us have a hard time believing it and knowing it to be the truth and nothing but the truth? Raise your hand again… Yeah, it's beyond me how in the world we ended up here. Well, I do have an idea and in short I'll just say that there are some people in our world who would prefer if humans didn't know just HOW powerful and divine they truly are because *empowered individuals who know themselves cannot be controlled;* and that is really bad for business.

Just look around you. Do you ever see any messages (tv, movies, newspapers, magazines, and music) telling you how great you are? Telling you that you are a child of God and as such you must Love yourSelf and treat yourSelf kindly? As of now, the mainstream media is filled with brainwashing messages to make us believe we are not good enough and on top of that, there always seems to be something outside of yourSelf that can fix you, fill you up and make you happy… Until the next thing… and the next one. But where does it end?

Well, it ends when YOU get to receive your undivided attention. It ends when you know that ALL of you is a magnificent, brilliant creation and you start acting accordingly. It sure does take *radical* Self-Love because we've been quite radical going in the other direction. We've been conditioned to occupy ourselves with so much nonsense just so we can be distracted; distracted from the truth. Because **when individuals are preoccupied with nonsense, they are blind to their own true power.** However, when we recognize the divinity of our human existence, Life radically changes.

Ask and you shall receive…
(Even if you didn't know you were asking for it)

So going back to my yoga practice… Embracing that practice into my Life was a big catalyst for me. I got hooked very quickly and found mySelf coming back to that heated room six and even seven times a week. That's an average of 540 minutes a week of looking at mySelf in the mirror. I'll be real with you and say that the reason I even started Bikram yoga was because I had heard it was a great "workout" where you can burn calories and get in shape. And that's all I needed to hear… Sign me up!

As time went by, thanks to my diligent practice (and devotion), things started to shift. I didn't only experience dramatic changes in my body, I also started noticing many other shifts in my Life. There was more peace. More clarity. I felt different on the inside. After a while I actually started to like what I was seeing in the mirror which was very surprising to me. It was as if I were seeing mySelf for the first time. Which was true; I was seeing mySelf through a new lense. A more loving lense. I didn't know all of that back then, I just knew I was having a very powerful experience which made me curious and eager to find out what else was possible.

Mind you, I wasn't looking for any profound awakening, I just wanted to get a good workout so I could look better in those tiny shorts. I didn't go to yoga class every day seeking for spirituality or enlightenment, and I definitely wasn't thinking about loving mySelf in the process. Now I know, as I look back, that even though my quest for Self-Love was disguised as a relentless obsession to look better, it was indeed my soul pulling me in the direction of my highest destiny; because the soul works in mysterious and very clever ways.

There are probably things you are consciously looking to shift in your Life which, with devotion, will naturally happen. It just works like that. And then, there are shifts that will take place without you even knowing you were needing them; but your soul sure knows. We do get what we want (sometimes), but we definitely *always get what we need* – whether we seek it or not.

Your inner world is the first thing to shift; then the rest follows. You'll start noticing how you're living your Life differently – from the choices you make, to your thoughts, attitudes, reactions, feelings, and priorities. You might be very surprised at times, just like I was when for the first time I actually liked my image in the mirror. You'll start seeing yourSelf and everything else through a different lense – almost as if seeing yourSelf and the world for the first time; just like a fresh new-born baby.

I have come such a long way since that day I walked into my first Bikram yoga class. Self-Love was not a concept I was familiar with neither was Self-Mastery. But I had the most important thing I needed in order to be where I am today – I was committed. And I'm still committed. I'm still devoted and will forever be devoted because this is a lifelong journey. Falling in Love with yourSelf, just as with Self-Mastery, is not the end result. It's a continuous exploration where you keep falling deeper and deeper in Love with yourSelf which in turn, strengthens your devotion to creating the best, most wholesome, and most fulfilling Life you can live.

Try this one on:

Rise in Love with the person in the mirror

Start a new habit of looking at yourSelf in the mirror **every day** and shower yourSelf with words of Love and appreciation. Tell yourSelf how amazing you are and how much you Love YOU. It might not be the easiest thing to do, maybe extremely awkward and uncomfortable, but that's the whole point. You want to change your belief system about yourSelf, your Self-worth, and your ability to Love and appreciate yourSelf in the same way you would your best friend, child, partner or the person you Love the most. Start little by little and use whatever words feel the most authentic to you. But be courageous enough to say 'I Love you' to yourSelf in the mirror *every single day*. You might begin by saying it once and walk away but with each passing day, you'll be able to do it for longer and eventually, you'll start loving up on yourSelf with juicy compliments, words of appreciation, and declarations of unconditional Love. *Look deeply into your eyes in the mirror and see your own divinity looking back at you with complete acceptance and compassion.* Allow yourSelf to rise in Love with who you are; inside and out.

You can take it a step further but only do it if you feel ready since it can be quite edgy for many. Don't push yourSelf to do the following if you know it's too much for you at this time; I know I had to build my way towards it. For this one, you'll do the same as above only standing in front of a full length mirror **completely naked.** I can't even tell you how beautiful, healing, and extremely empowering it will be for you, especially if you used to have or perhaps still dealing with body image issues. Being bold enough to do this will dramatically shift the way you perceive yourSelf and your body. This practice will help you create a new level of intimacy in your Life, increasing your ability to be truly intimate with yourSelf and with other people as well; and by intimacy I mean closeness, affection, and warmth. Intimacy is simply the ability to see into another and be vulnerable enough to be fully seen by them. In this case here, we're looking to develop your ability to fully be seen by you and fully see into yourSelf affectionately and with a loving heart.

YOUR RELATIONSHIP WITH YOURSELF NEEDS YOU TO BE THERE

Priorities is the name of the game here – to learn how to prioritize your Life and put yourSelf on the top of the list. Who knows, this might be the first time for you. If it is, definitely give yourSelf time to reorganize your priorities. Like I've mentioned earlier, there are some things we can shift relatively quickly but with most things, especially deep rooted habits and patterns, slow and steady wins the race (or the journey because it's definitely not a race).

Now, a word about being a busy bee as I'm sure many of you are:

Hiding behind being busy is merely an excuse to not take care of your-Self.

There, I said it.

Do you really want to tell me that you're too busy to be in this one in a Lifetime relationship?? (Which is quite hilarious because you don't really have a choice when it comes to that... Nowhere to go, remember?)

I've seen it time and again and continue to see it all around me. Whether you are an entrepreneur or have a nine to five, whether you are the CEO of your own company or a full time mom, achieving "out there" or taking care of others is not your only mission here on Earth. You must achieve "in there" as well – that is, your own domain made out of your body, mind, heart, and soul. Some people use their busy schedule as a way to avoid taking care of themselves. It's one of the most prevalent programs we've been subjected to in our society. We've been conditioned to believe that the "out there" is more important and in some cases, the only thing that is important.

But when you TRULY Love yourSelf and realize how precious and important your vessel is, how can you do that?

So the first step is to develop that kind of a foundation for yourSelf. You can have the busiest schedule on the planet and still create time to care for yourSelf; that's just a simple matter of priorities. And when you change your priorities according to what you deem to be important, you'll find a way to fit it in. It can be the tiniest thing at first. We're all at different stages on our journey so turn up the Love volume on yourSelf in whichever way you can. If you didn't invest time and energy in your other relationships, if there isn't a genuine demonstration of Love and care, that relationship will eventually deteriorate. So unless you want your Life and well-being to deteriorate, I'd say, get your priorities straight.

Alongside your commitment to giving more Love and attention to your-

Self, you also want to cultivate **consistency.** It's one thing to be committed and devoted, and it's a whole other story to be consistent. It makes sense to have consistency with something you are committed to, yes, but that's not always the case. I've found that developing the ability to be consistent works in the same way as developing a muscle in your body. If it's quite weak, well, you'll need to really zoom in on that specific muscle and make sure you develop it enough so it can support the rest of your structure.

As with your body, which works as a complete unit, if you have a weak muscle (or pretty much anything else – organ, joint, gland, bone, etc.), other things will be compromised as a result. The more fundamental that part of your body is, the more it will affect the rest. For example, a malfunctioning heart or brain impacts your overall well-being more than a broken pinky (from a wholistic perspective, even that little pinky can have a pretty significant impact, but we can all agree on what is more critical and fundamental).

Being consistent with your commitment to yourSelf is fundamental. It's crucial for you to be consistent with your actions and practical applications. If the Love you develop for yourSelf is the heart of your mastery journey, your consistency acts as your spine. Some have a very strong spine, others a very weak one, and the majority fall somewhere in the middle of the spectrum. If you know that consistency is one of your weaker links, please don't try to force yourSelf into being more consistent. Beating yourSelf up is not the approach we're going for.

Instead, since it all ties together and very much connected, all you need to focus on is prioritizing your Life in a way that honors your well-being.

A way that demonstrates your Love for yourSelf. More consistency will naturally emerge as a result of that. You'll actually start wanting to do the things you might have been struggling to be consistent with – that's one of the greatest shifts you will experience. And quite naturally; like the shift from discipline to devotion.

Choose what is doable (and stick to it)

This is the golden key to staying consistent. Choose what you know is doable for you. Taking on too much is actually a way to sabotage our own commitment since our success relies on our consistently. Doable doesn't necessarily mean comfortable or not challenging. You can very well challenge yourSelf with new things to embody while staying in your personal doable zone. Sometimes, we can feel so inspired and motivated to implement a bunch of awesome practices into our daily routine that it gets to be too overwhelming. As a result, we end up not doing any of it. Does that sound familiar? Or we might do all of those awesome things for a few weeks until it all starts to fade away because it's too much to handle. Being too heroic in a moment of inspiration only to end up losing steam causes us to feel defeated; to feel bad about ourselves which leads to lack of consistency. That my friend, is one of the most toxic cycles you can drag yourSelf into. It will completely suck all the air from under your wings so let's nip it in the bud, shall we?

Since I offer a lot of different tools in this book, I'd like to emphasize the importance of picking only what is doable for you. Don't take it all on, only to realize later it's not realistic and is actually causing you more stress than anything else. That's definitely not the point. Choosing what is doable is imperative to how consistent you'll be able to be. Choosing what is doable will ensure your long term success and that's what we want. Not just the feel good for a month then forget all about it.

What is considered to be doable for you will change (and most likely expand) over time. Just begin from where you're at right now and let the journey naturally progress and show you when it's time to step it up. And yes, you might need to nudge yourSelf every once in awhile to step out of your comfort zone and try something new but nevertheless, stick to what you know is doable for you.

Even if you start with the tiniest thing, as long as you know it's doable, something you can do every day, grab it and run with it! Don't sabotage your own success and fulfillment by polluting yourSelf with unnecessary judgments about your capabilities. When a child takes their first step you celebrate them, you don't tell the child 'Come on dummy, you better start running soon!' Sounds ridiculous but so often we do that to ourselves, setting ourselves up for inevitable let down. Over here at "Self-Love land", we are choosing to use a different approach, a more loving and compassionate approach – and a much more effective one

At times, you will need to employ the maturity of your tough Love (similarly to a loving parent) when it's time for you to rearrange your priorities and take important steps in the direction of your ultimate well-being. However, there's a big difference between being harshly critical and being lovingly discerning what is or isn't so great for your Life.

If you know you can do more, then by all means, be honest with yourSelf and expand your "doable zone". One of my teachers used to always say, *If you can, you must*. It's your job to know what is in the realm of your "I can" so don't give yourSelf any excuses if you know there's more you can give yourSelf. Remember to Love that part of you who wants to say "I can't" (because we all have it) and continue to raise up the bar anyway. After all, this is between you and yourSelf.

Choose what is doable.
Be consistent with it.
Allow the miracles to happen.

BUILDING YOUR FOUNDATION
Essential building blocks

We can agree that our human experience is very interesting and rich. Throughout our Life's journey we are faced with a wide range of emotions, thoughts, challenging conflicts (internal and external), tough decisions, unexpected events, sudden changes, great achievements, great loses, tremendous joy and tremendous pain. A variety of earthquakes can occur at any given moment – from emotional earthquakes to mental earthquakes, physical earthquakes, spiritual earthquakes and sometimes all of the above happening at the same time. But the one thing that is constant no matter how much is moving and shaking within or around you, is YOU.

When your relationship with yourSelf is unshakably solid, even the strongest earthquake cannot and will not take you down; you might be taken down physically, mentally or emotionally, but your soul will always guide you back up so if and when you do go down, you pick yourSelf back up very quickly, put a smile on your face and continue to move forward. You will get shaken from time to time, yes, but you won't get destroyed; that's how resilient and invincible your soul is. The more you connect to it and become one with it by developing a strong relationship with yourSelf, the more you'll be able to truly master your Life.

With the understanding that your relationship with yourSelf is in fact your foundation, the number one thing to support the structure of your Life, we can now move on to the essential building blocks of the foundation itself. Let each building block be a part of your unshakable foundation as each of the following elements plays an integral role in your upgraded relationship with yourSelf and Life as a whole. The following sections contain many practical applications – tools for you to use on a regular basis. Even a new attitude or a belief about yourSelf can be considered a tool. A new attitude about who you think you are or what you perceive Life to be can be a catalyst for creating radical shifts in your Life. Keep your mind open, your heart open, and most importantly, let your inner wisdom guide the way…

Building Block #1: Accepting & Allowing

How often have you heard the terms: *Just accept what is,* or *Accept who you are*? But what the heck does it mean? How do I accept mySelf if there are things I want to change? If I accept what is, does that mean I like it? Does it mean I need to force mySelf to like it? Does it mean I need to accept unacceptable conditions and just deal with it?

Let's begin by looking at the actual definition of acceptance:

- *The action of consenting to receive or undertake something offered.*
- *The process or fact of being received as adequate, valid, or suitable.*

Some of the synonymous words for acceptance are: *Welcoming, Favourable, Reception, Embracing, Approval, Adoption, Integration*

'Accepting what is' is merely an attitude; a mindset to live by rather than a black and white fact. The basic premise of this attitude is that we can't control Life. Unexpected or unpredictable occurrences are a part of Life and many times these are events or situations we wouldn't necessarily choose to experience if we had any say in the matter.

By accepting what is you choose to believe that no matter what is taking place in your Life – the good, the bad, and the ugly – Life **always** has your best interest at heart. Now, it is easy to celebrate that fact when wonderful events take place in our lives; no problem. We can easily accept whatever is occurring within and around us as long as it goes according to our "plan". However, are you still able to accept and even celebrate the things in Life which might not be as pleasant? Do you still accept what Life is offering you even when things are not going your way or when shit really hits the fan?

There have been numerous occasions in my Life when I **really** didn't like what was happening at the time. I had a desire for a certain outcome but Life seemed to have a different idea than mine; I'm sure I'm not alone here. Most of us have experienced that more than once. The amount of disappointment and frustration that comes with those experiences can be heartbreaking and exhausting. And why do we feel frustrated or upset? Because if it's not matching our personal agenda, we have a hard time accepting what is taking place. However, when we look back at those ex-periences, we realize just how vital they were and we actually end up being grateful for it all.

Fortunately, over time, I've learned to give Life a bit more credit by ac-cepting that which is taking place *in the moment* rather than in retrospect; no matter how disappointing or undesirable the experience may be. By adopting this approach, I save mySelf a great deal of frustration and tur-moil because I choose to believe that Life has my back.

The attitude of acceptance recognizes that EVERYTHING is a blessing. Every experience becomes a gift.

Just to give you the heads up, your logical mind and ego are going to battle this statement with everything they got. Don't fight it back. Your only job is to keep trusting Life a tad more (or a lot more!).

Now, It's important to be honest with how you feel so accepting something doesn't mean you pretend to like it or suppress whatever emotions get stirred up for you. The mindset of **acceptance is not be used as a way to suppress your true feelings;** it's merely a lens in which to view Life. We can be honest with ourselves and others and admit we really don't like our current experience (if that's the truth) and at the same time, not push against it.

The way we respond to Life – whether it be different circumstances, different emotions, personality traits, other people, etc, is a choice. You get to CHOOSE how to respond; moment by moment. What really determines the quality of your experiences is not the actual experience, but the way you choose to interact with it. Pushing against a certain experience or wishing it wouldn't happen is equivalent to you pushing against a big wave in the ocean. If you've ever had the "pleasure" of being tumbled under one of those, you know what I'm talking about.

You fight it and you'll lose your breath. You fight it and it will take you down again and again. You fight it and you'll get exhausted and scared. But, if you say, oh boy, there's a big wave coming and just relax into it, even though you might be scared to your core, the wave will eventually carry you back to shore... At the very least, it will take you on a heck of a ride with you feeling exhilarated rather than exhausted and out of breath.

Start adopting this mindset in your Life with every unpleasant experience or big scary wave and watch your mental, emotional (and even physical) well-being transform.

With all that being said, let's talk about what I call unacceptable conditions because the attitude of 'accepting what is' can be taken to the extreme by some people. Let me be very clear. If you find yourSelf in situations where you are not being honored, valued, accepted, loved, respected, appreciated or even safe and **you have the power** to remove yourSelf from that situation or change the circumstances (have it be a relationship, a job, an interaction, an environment, etc.), you don't just accept what is and go with it. Like with the wave analogy, if the waters are extremely rough, don't even get in. And if you're already in and it feels like a bad idea, get the hell out of there as soon as you can.

The base line is always your well-being and Self-worth. If something doesn't match that base line, it has no room in your Life. Accepting what is doesn't mean you become a floor mat. That is non-negotiable.

After clearing that, what about accepting and welcoming your **internal experiences?** ALL of them. We can get so lost in our quest for Self-development that we forget our real humanness. I can tell you from my own personal experience that for a very long time I had an internal struggle every time I felt less than elated or full of joy. I thought there was something wrong with me or that I wasn't doing something right simply because I felt sadness or not so cheerful. That was my way of not accepting what is in that moment because I believed I was supposed to feel a certain way all the time. It's the fighting and pushing against *any specific experience,* whether it be internal or external that brings about unnecessary struggle and actually prolongs the process. In simple terms this is what we call suffering. Unpleasant experiences don't have to equate suffering. How we choose to respond to the experience will determine that factor.

Put this in your tool box:

> From now on, during moments of undesirable or unpleasant situations and experiences, whether it be the way you feel or what's happening around you, practice opening your heart and arms and say:
>
> 'Thank you _____ (whatever feeling, experience, thought, fear, etc). I welcome you into my Life. What are you here to show me?'
>
> Then be open to receive and be shown no matter how uncomfortable the answer may be...

This statement places you in a receptive seat, willing and open to embrace whatever the moment is presenting to you (and again, I'm not talking about extreme situations where conditions are unacceptables).

This attitude is essential when you're facing deeply rooted patterns of yours. Are there patterns you possess but desperately want to shift? Have you been "working" on it for a while? Have you ever tried, maybe only for a moment, to accept that about yourSelf and, (let me take it one step further), Love that about yourSelf? Or has your approach been mostly one of pushing, denying, condemning, and avoiding? Are you able to actually see that everything within you, everything that makes you who you are is part of the miracle that is you?

The first necessary step we need to take in the direction of real change is changing our attitude – from condemning to accepting. Otherwise, the recipe works like this: *Whatever we resist persists.* So if you desire to create a better relationship with yourSelf and to dissolve the persistence of undesirable patterns, you first must welcome them. By welcoming these patterns, we also acknowledge they have something to show us. So instead of pushing the patterns away by condemning them, just keep looking closer and closer in order to see what they have to offer you…

We may fear that if we accept something (especially our own destructive patterns), they will want to stick around forever. But the opposite is true. Accepting something doesn't mean you let it become a permanent resident in your reality. Accepting and welcoming it in simply gives it the attention it's calling for. Once you give your attention to it, the shifts will occur naturally and effortlessly without any struggle and forceful attempts to push it out of your reality.

Acceptance makes you a willing, open, and active participant in the play of Life; and you get to choose HOW to play it.

To continue with the theme of accepting what is, let's go a step further into what I like to call "Allowing". This is one of my favorite words in the english language. There's something so soothing about it… Say it outloud. Feel it in your body. *I allow.* Doesn't it feel good??

On my quest to find out the definition of this fantastic word, I found some words which are the opposite of allowing. Feel the difference in your body when reading or saying these words: *Deny, reject, disapprove, forbid, refuse, resist.* Doesn't feel as good, does it? Yet, very often we put ourselves in those states, consciously or not. The trick is to recognize when (and why) you find yourSelf in one of those shady neighborhoods and get yourSelf out of there as quickly as possible. Being in a state of disallowing (or any of the other equivalent states above), can be a result of several different factors.

Let us explore…

Allowing goes hand in hand with accepting, which is why I put them together. We can look at acceptance as the first step, the opening act before 'allowing' gets the proper space on the stage of your Life. If we are still stuck in fighting what is, there is no way we can allow that which is wanting to enter our reality.

To demonstrate what allowing means, imagine a hose that is connected to a water source. You are the hose and the water is Life; the natural flow of Life. As long as the hose is free of any restrictions, the water flows freely through it. Get the hose all knotted up, tangled, or constricted in any way and the water (Life's flow) has no way to move. It gets stuck and at some point, will blow up.

How do we as humans constrict the hose? Well, pushing against Life is one way. Whenever something unwanted happens in our lives (especially when it's unpredictable), our first instinct is to contract; which is quite natural when looking at Life from a limited perspective. As a human being, when being primarily guided by the ego, all we see is survival. The ego's agenda is to stay safe and protected so anything which threatens that status quo is deemed to be a dangerous enemy and must be fought against. For the ego (or in our limited perspective), the known and familiar is what we consider safe and the unknown, or the unfamiliar, unsafe.

You've been working for the same company for 20 years (known and safe) and now they're letting you go; you've been in a relationship with the Love of your Life for many years (known and safe) and now they've decided to go in a different direction… without you; you've lived in the same house for years (known and safe) and now you've received a 30-day notice to move out. Just a few examples of Life's twists and turns. I'm sure we've all had our fair share of those experiences and will continue to experience the unpredictable throughout our lives.

But here's what's so essential to remember: **Life is not happening to you, it's happening FOR you.**

Life is always seeking to evolve. Just look around you… There's constant change happening all the time. Everywhere. As a vehicle of Life's flow, as a cell in the body of Life, (yes, that's you), if you don't initiate change every once in awhile or if you get too stagnant in your own bubble (either internally, externally, or both), Life itself will arrange the change for you – starting with a tap on the shoulder, which sometimes, when ignored, turns into a two-by-four just to get your attention.

It is the power of your soul working to move and steer you in a certain direction. A direction you never have imagined perhaps. If the ego sees Life from a limited perspective of survival and goals, the soul sees Life from a broader vantage point; it sees a bigger picture which is not obvious to us from our limited view. Our ego sits in the valley while our soul is standing on the mountain top. Which of the two has the ability to have a better view of the entire landscape? Which of the two are you going to listen to when you're not able to see the full picture yet?

That's when ALLOWING comes in.

We've already covered the futility of fighting what is – the fact that we do it only because our known zone, our safe zone is being threatened; the frustration we feel when things aren't going "our way". In our limited point of view, we don't have all the information right here and now. However, after giving our ego a good training we start seeing that Life, (as it's working side by side with our soul), is indeed moving us in a different direction we weren't necessarily planning on. Fighting the present moment is **rejecting** what is taking place. By fighting it, you're **refusing** to accept what Life is offering you. By fighting it, you're **resisting** the natural flow of Life. But when you drop the fight and say yes to the unknown, you ALLOW fresh energy into your Life. When you stop resisting, Life can gift you that which you couldn't see from your ego's point of view deep down in the valley.

Our ability to release the constricting fight and allow Life's flow to move through the hose again, gives Life the opportunity and the necessary time to unfold in the most wondrous (and very often mysterious) ways. Your soul sees endless possibilities while your ego (and logical mind) sees only one way on a very narrow path. It's your job to start listening to the whispers of your soul more often... And trust me, it's not going to make sense most of the time. Can you allow it though?

The same thing applies to your internal reality. For example, if for many years you've identified yourSelf with being a social butterfly (let's say, an extreme extrovert) but all of a sudden you feel like you're needing and wanting more time alone, don't fight it. If staying at home reading a book on a Saturday night is the most exciting thing on your list, honor that rather than ignoring or judging your needs. Your inner world shifts just as much as your external world and we must learn how to allow those internal changes to occur without the struggle. This might be an obvious thing yet, I encounter many people, in my personal Life and in my work with clients, who struggle when their inner reality shifts; especially if it's a big shift. The voice of the good old "should" kicks in and you start having an internal battle with yourSelf. Wouldn't it be a lot easier to just allow yourSelf to be whatever Life is asking you to be?

Some people actually have a harder time with this one than with any external changes. Some may call it an identity crisis. Let's face it, the shifts will happen, like it or not. Your inner world, just as your outer world, is not stagnant. Allowing the shifts to occur naturally, letting your soul take you from one inner world to the next, will reveal to you so much more of who you truly are – but you must allow yourSelf to be what you feel is right for you; allow yourSelf to do what it is you want to do rather than what you think you "should do"; allow yourSelf to listen to your inner voice of the present moment rather than the voice of who you once were.

Allow yourSelf to be who you are while accepting the changeable nature of reality. Don't "should" on yourSelf and definitely don't let anyone else "should" on you.

When approaching the natural shifts within you in this way, an identity crisis can become a celebrated rebirth. It might be scary, definitely uncomfortable, but on the other side of that is a new you and more often than not, a new you means a new Life.

Hold on to the old and be dragged. Allow the new to take form and be lifted to unimaginable heights.

Try this one on:

You can do this process either by yourSelf, with a close friend or your significant other.

- Write or speak **out loud** everything that you feel stressed out about, anxious, fearful, confused, frustrated, disappointment, unclear, etc.

  Or, in the same way as above, you can state whichever unpleasant Life experience, situation, event or big change (internally or externally) you are currently experiencing and what is it bringing up for you – how are you feeling as a result.

- Sit with all that you're feeling for **at least 90 seconds** (can be more but not less) and **fully feel it**. If there's anywhere specific in your body you're experiencing the feeling, notice that. Acknowledge what it is you're feeling in your body – any sensations or tension. There's no right or wrong. Whatever is being felt by you is for you to experience and be with. Speak whatever arises out loud and/or write it down.

  By allowing yourSelf to feel your feelings you are actually transforming them. When you avoid feeling your true feelings or when judging them harshly, you stay stuck in the patterns of the ego. This takes practice but with time, you'll start feeling more comfortable with being with what is without avoiding or running away. By doing that, you'll start seeing the gift within each uncomfortable feeling or Life situation, freeing yourSelf from unnecessary internal and external conflicts.

- Say this statement out loud, either to yourSelf or to the other person: "I acknowledge this _____ (stress, fear, anxiety, confusion, sadness, frustration, hurt, uncertainty, etc.) as a gift and I RECEIVE it here as I am now."

- Take a deep breath in, hold it for a few seconds, then a long exhale out.

- Say the statement: "God/Spirit/Universe/My higher Self (use whatever term resonates with you), I release this ___ (stress, fear, anxiety, confusion, sadness, frustration, etc.) back to you. Thank you for helping me **recognize, feel, and receive** this so I can see mySelf more clearly and return to Love."

- Deep breath in again, hold it for a few seconds, then a long exhale out.

- Notice the relief in your body. Place your hands on your heart and say silently or out loud: "I Love you. I am so amazing and powerful. Thank you, Thank you, Thank you." *(If you are doing it with a partner, just let the other person witness you as you are)*

- You can journal about your experience and what you've learned from it.

Building Block #2: Be Authentic & Be Sovereign

As we address our emotional wounds by embracing our inner child, we automatically gain more confidence to truly be ourselves; to fully express ourselves and live more authentically and truthfully. When you start to accept and Love yourSelf, you naturally free yourSelf from any need to pretend, hide, compete or fake it in any way. When you truly know you are good enough (and more than just good enough, you know that you and everyone else is a miracle of divine wisdom), why would you need to pretend to be anything else? Or to compete with anyone else? Or to compare yourSelf to anyone else?

Knowing that you are indeed a divine miracle also helps you gain the ability to be a sovereign being – to be your own source of power and authority rather than letting other people, governments, corporations, religions, or trends dictate how you should or shouldn't live your Life. When we do that, we unknowingly fall into the trap of pretending to be something we are not just because we fear the consequences. That mind set takes away your authentic expression and your sovereignty which are ultimately your source of personal power and freedom. And I'm talking about *True Freedom* which can only be sourced from within. *It's a state of being rather than something you feel as a result of external Life conditions.*

More often than not, we do these things unconsciously. You don't wake up in the morning saying: *Today I am going to put on a mask and hide how I truly feel and who I truly am...* Or: *Today I am going to compete with the rest of the world because I feel insecure and don't believe in my own capabilities...* Or: *Today I am going to give my power away because I don't trust mySelf and don't think I'm good enough...* These behavioural patterns are repeated throughout Life as a result of emotional wounds that have been sitting in the dark and running the show on our behalf.

When you are focused on creating the most loving and truthful relationship with yourSelf, you ultimately pave the way to living a Life of true freedom accompanied by a sense of sovereignty; a sense of supreme inner power and inner authority. This also leads to living a Life of integrity – being in integrity with yourSelf, first and foremost, which results in holding the highest standard of integrity when dealing with other people and with Life in general. And what is integrity? *Integrity is the quality of being honest and having strong moral principles.* **The state of being whole and undivided.** *(Honesty, Honour, Ethics, Morality, Decency, Fairness, Sincerity, Truthfulness, Trustworthiness, Unification, Wholeness, Coherence, Cohesion)* – just a few synonymous words.

Living authentically requires us to live in integrity; it's quite impossible to separate the two. **The more integrity we cultivate within ourselves, the more we'll be able to live authentically.** When we're not authentic with other people, when we put on a mask just so we can be perceived a certain way or so we can get our way, we are not being honest; we're not being sincere. In that moment we step away from our integrity, not honoring our commitment to ourselves. It's really important to remember the interconnectedness between your integrity and your authenticity if you want to build your relationship with yourSelf (and with others) on a strong and reliable foundation. And that's what we're going for, right?

In our world today, neither authenticity or sovereignty are encouraged. There's so much fakeness around us, so much deception and illusion, it's hard to distinguish between the real and the fake, the true and the false. We are being bombarded with endless stream of messages telling us what we should do, what we should wear, how we should act, what we should eat, who we should marry… On top of that, it always seems like "whoever" is out there knows better than you and has the power over your Life. Anything to steer you in the opposite direction of your own true power (sovereignty) and unique expression (authenticity). But what is the motive behind this, you might ask? Well, when humans feel small and powerless, they can be easily controlled. That's the motive.

This crazy cycle stops when you learn how to live authentically as a sovereign being. That is the antidote. That's how we empower ourselves as individuals and as a collective.

Most of what I offer in this book takes practice, yes, but this one is especially tricky and requires our undivided attention and dedication. It will vary from person to person but at the end of the day, we all put our masks on – different masks at different times, and we can all fall into the trap of pretending to be something we're not. It sure is a trap but we can powerfully notice the trap and choose not to fall into it. When you start using your authenticity meter on a regular basis, you'll become more sensitive to what's real and what's not; within yourSelf and around you. You'll become a bullshit detective as I like to call it, but first, you must recognize when you're bullshiting yourSelf.

I Love those moments when I get super real and call mySelf out on my own BS. I actually laugh now. Yes, I laugh at mySelf (or with mySelf) because it's absolutely humorous to observe the ways in which we try to deceive ourselves, the ways in which we mask who we truly are or how we truly feel; the ways we give our power away (as subtle as it may be). The moment you adjust who you are or bend your truth in accordance to someone else, you step away from your authentic expression and hence, step away from your inner authority, integrity, and power.

The trick is to catch it in the moment (or soon after), learn the valuable lesson, and do something different next time. The invitation is to always be radically honest with yourSelf – honest about how you feel, your likes and dislikes, your wants and needs, your true heart desires, your fears, your views of the world, what's true or not true for you. It's very empowering when we get real with ourselves and notice if and when we are bending or completely covering our truth because of fear – the fear of not getting or losing whichever it is we deem worthy enough to mask ourselves for.

In most cases, we put on different masks and pull our authenticity off the main stage when there's a "target" in front of us; a desirable goal we want to achieve or conquer. Whether the goal is to get the girl or the guy, to get the job, to get the approval of others, to feel included in something or just to feel like you belong, when you look deeper, all those different desires stem from the same root: *we just want to feel loved. We want to feel safe.* It always comes back to the same basic needs we all share as human beings. And there's nothing wrong with that. We are human. What I want to tell you though, is this:

Take off the masks and stop pretending, because who you are is good enough. In fact, who you *truly* are is the BEST.

Unfortunately, many of us have been conditioned to think that in order to be liked or loved we need to hide who we truly are. We need to censor our feelings, thoughts and words, and most certainly, our uniqueness. Because if you want to "fit in", you must be like everyone else, even if that means you need to fake it. Even if that means you are going to disregard what feels true to you and let someone else be responsible for your Life. I don't think there's a better way to suck a person's Life force out of them. To not live authentically and as a sovereign being out of fear, (whatever the fear may be), is like a slow death for your heart and soul.

There aren't any special tools for this one. It simply requires your awareness. You could start by making a list of different areas in your Life where you feel you are:

1. Out of integrity – with yourSelf and/or in your relationships.

2. Not being authentic by pretending one way or another or by not being true to yourSelf.

3. Giving external sources the authority to tell you how to live your Life. (That can be family, partners, friends, co-workers, the church, society, etc.)

Once you know what needs to be adjusted, you can then take the necessary steps. As always, be patient with this process and continue to employ your dedication to yourSelf and your well-being. Being free from wearing masks or blindly following someone else's instructions is going to take your well-being onto a whole other level and place your innate power back to where it belongs.

Building Block #3: Who are you living for? Your Personal Guidance system – Learning Discernment & Healthy Boundaries

As you are creating a stronger and more loving relationship with yourSelf, you will start to appreciate the extreme value of having personal boundaries and the ability to discern what does or doesn't have room in your Life by relying exclusively on your personal guidance system. To do that, we first must know what works for us, what nurtures us and what depletes us. As we redefine our relationship with ourselves, we also start to redefine that which we truly value and desire in Life, recognizing what does or doesn't fit that.

Discerning what is truly the highest and setting healthy boundaries accordingly can be a challenging task for some. More often than not, this challenge is a result of disregarding one's personal guidance system, one's own internal compass. Many people live under the impression that being a loving person means they must say 'yes' to every request or that they must cater to everyone else. When one believes that other people's happiness and fulfillment is somehow dependent on what they choose to do, there's a drive to provide what others expect of them. It can be a slippery slope – a fine line between being of service to others and sacrificing one's values and personal well-being.

The way I choose to approach this slippery slope is by using the same principle in every situation: *keeping my overall well-being as top priority.* As long as I stick to **what feels true to me in the moment** (aka, my guidance system), I trust I am being of service to everyone else *even* if that means I need to say no to someone or something, end a relationship or a contract, walk away from something, or simply make any changes I deem to be necessary. This definitely becomes more challenging when we are dealing with our close circle – family, partners, business partners, friends, etc. but ultimately, the one you're always dealing with is yourSelf, so this is who you must stay true to and nurture above all else.

We each have our own internal compass but because we are all connected, we can't separate one internal compass from another. This doesn't mean we all have the same compass or that all of our compasses point in the same direction at all times. What it means is that the direction my compass is showing me is ONLY for me to follow; and while it's only for me to follow, it is also directly connected to other compasses and the direction they're pointing. So how does it work?

Since you can't control others' compasses (nor does anyone else have the right to interfere with your personal compass), your one and only responsibility is to TRUST and FOLLOW your own compass. You must remember that any choice you make at any given moment, when based on what you know to be right for you, is serving everyone else involved (even when other people might be disappointed, let down, maybe even hurt). You never want to hurt anybody for the sake of hurting them, of course not, but the bottom line is that disappointment and pain is part of Life we all experience one way or another.

When we lack a sense of discernment or healthy boundaries, we can get caught up in the loop of wanting to spare someone from an unpleasant situation or feeling, making it impossible to say 'no'. Even though it's coming from a very loving place, it is extremely disempowering for both parties and is actually robbing both yourSelf and the other person of what could be an important experience. Doing that ends up not only causing pain to ourselves (there's nothing more painful for your heart and soul than the pain of you turning against your true guidance), but also hindering another person's opportunity to learn and grow.

If you look back at your Life, hasn't every devastating or unpleasant experience ended up being a catalyst for something greater? Being on the receiving end of those experiences, if there was another person (or people) involved, we can really thank them for following what felt true for them in that moment. By sticking to their personal voice of discernment and guidance they actually set us free – free to move forward into the next chapter of our lives.

Next time you find yourSelf on the other side of this equation, when being faced with tough choices, maybe even guilt and concern for someone else's welfare; when you are the one who needs to break the hard news to someone (and yes, there's a sensitive and respectful way to go about it) – if your guidance system speaks to you loud and clear, if you undoubtedly know what is the right course of action, **follow it with conviction.**

If you need to say 'no' to something or someone because it doesn't feel like the right path to choose or to continue on, it's crucial you do that. You will be freeing so much energy for yourSelf and the other person (or people) whatever the situation may be. Discerning what is or isn't right for you allows other doors to open up. More suitable doors. Doors that will lead you (and others) to more fulfilling paths. That's how powerful our interconnectedness is. *What we may deem as "selfish" is actually in the highest service of all.*

> **"Somehow or another, the human race has colluded to create the idea that Life is about something other than living for ourselves. We've got to be responsible providers, achieve, succeed, become famous, look good, be great lovers, and sacrifice ourselves. Who's bloody Life is it, though? That's all our conditioning. It's all for someone else. It's all about getting stuck on some objective and occupying your time with that while Life passes you by. Society holds out meaningless objectives and says, 'this is the point', and we blindly attach ourselves to it."**
>
> *- 'The Magician Way' by William Whitecloud*

Living for yourSelf doesn't suggests you don't care about anybody else. When you know how to set healthy boundaries based on your personal guidance system, you actually give others permission to do the same. That alone, immediately empowers that individual and puts the power back in their hands. Isn't that being of service to someone much more than accommodating their immediate desire, request, or comfort zone just because you don't want to either disappoint them or seem like the "bad guy"? If we keep doing the latter, we'll be forever stuck in a loop of personal disempowerment, mutual disabling, fear based decisions and lack of true fulfillment.

The truth is, it's not your job to make anyone else happy nor is it anyone else's responsibility to make you happy. We are each responsible for our own quality of Life because it all starts from within; everyone and every-thing else is the icing on the cake. You must learn to distinguish between service and sacrifice; how to discern between that which uplifts and in-spires you and that which depletes your vital Life force. That can show up in the form of people you spend time with, close relationships, different activities, jobs, personal habits, etc. Anything you invest time and energy in, anything you are in a relationship with, the first order of business is to ask yourSelf:

- Is this **enhancing** the quality of my Life or not?
- Does this **nourish and fulfill** me or not?
- Does this **increase and better** my well-being or not?

Our personal compass is always pointing us in the right direction; all we need to do is listen. Listen to what feels right for you. You can feel it in your body. You can feel it in your heart. If something doesn't feel true or right for you, your body will tend to contract and close down. That's your signal. If your heart feels heavy when being asked to do something, that's your inner guidance saying to move in a different direction. But if you are easily swayed by your environment, you'll keep compromising the most important thing you have in Life and that is you.

Let me give you an example from my own personal Life...

My mom was very unhappy being married to my dad. They got married young, and she pretty much wanted to bail out of that relationship soon after they'd had my oldest brother. But she was 21, with a newborn baby and in a new country. As opposed to today's world, back then in the early 70's, it wasn't as easy or even socially acceptable to end a marriage at such a young age. So on top of her personal fears, she was also facing the constrictive norms of society at that time. And so she stayed. Life circumstances appeared to be much bigger and louder than her own guidance system. It's not like she didn't know (because let's face it – we *always* know), she just chose not to listen, not to honor her well-being. (It's amazing how fear can make us turn our back on ourselves and paralyze us in the most astonishing ways).

She stayed in that marriage (and I must add, extremely dysfunctional and miserable marriage) for another 24 years. The desire to break free from that relationship and to say 'yes' to her heart's true calling were very much alive for her during all those years. But the fear of splitting the family, the fear of hurting the kids (especially me, since I was the youngest), the fear of starting again all alone were at the forefront of her decision making process; not her well-being and definitely not her personal guidance system. As a loving mother, she had my best interest at heart and a desire to protect me, to make sure I had a solid place to call home. The truth is, that environment was the last thing that felt solid to me... the last thing that felt loving or safe.

You see, when you go against what you feel and know is right for you, even if it's for the sake of someone else, you'll always end up unhappy and in most cases, quite resentful. Don't fool yourSelf and think that others can't sense your own unhappiness, unfulfillment, and misery. I sure did feel that in my mother and I sure did feel awful living under the same roof with a mother and a father who didn't speak with one another. Although her intention was to protect me, at the end of the day, that miserable reality she was living in created so much anguish for herself and everyone else. So when my mom told me she had decided to file for divorce, I couldn't be happier. I was 12 at that time and all I can remember is sitting there, thinking: "Thank God!"

And so finally, after almost 25 years of living against her guidance system, against her values and heart's desires, she conjured enough courage to set healthy boundaries for herself and said 'enough is enough'. She was able to step more fully into her sense of Self-worth (it always comes down to that) and acknowledge that she wanted something different; she finally acknowledged she deserved more. Fears can have a strong grip on us, yes, but when the feeling of dying on the inside becomes even stronger, it truly is unbearable to keep living in the same way for even another day.

I'm telling you this story to inspire you to take the action you feel guided to take, whatever it may be, however big or small. Maybe it is to file for that divorce, or maybe it's to have a tough and truthful conversation with someone regarding what is or isn't acceptable for you. Maybe you do need to set some clear boundaries with someone if you feel disrespected in some way or maybe it's time for something to end or to change and you must be the initiator, taking the first step in a new direction. Go back to those basic questions above and be honest about the quality you experience in all areas of your Life.

The initial step is always the hardest and the transition period can be quite challenging when you make a tough decision and put it into motion. It may take weeks, months, and sometimes years for harmony to be restored, but that's just part of Life. Don't let that stop you. Ultimately, it helps you and everyone else on their journey to live a more fulfilled Life driven by truth rather than fear.

My parents are best friends now, better than ever before. It took a few years, however, they now have the best relationship they've ever had. Who knows what would have happened if my mom did stay in that marriage. I cannot even imagine how miserable she would be today. Your Life is way too precious for that. People actually get sick and die after years and years of not listening to their personal guidance system because they want to maintain the status quo, to protect other people or to make sure others are happy; even if that means they're miserable. When people live like that long enough, their heart shrivels so much, it doesn't even have the energy to live anymore.

I'm thankful my mom took that step. For herself, first and foremost, and for everyone else. And I'm so proud of her too. That was a very courageous thing to do and it doesn't matter it took her 25 years to do so (hey, I wouldn't be here if it wasn't for that so everything always works out perfectly, right?)

At the end of the day, we all want ourselves and the people we Love to be happy. And yes, sometimes that means someone's happiness comes through our personal disappointment, a heartbreak or a divorce, and vice versa. But if we can accept the choices we and others need to make, we would be able to view Life from a higher perspective. Seeing Life choices from that higher perspective gives us the skill to honor our own and others' guidance systems and boundaries. Can you imagine how much more harmony we will experience individually, in our relationships, and collectively if we all start living by these values and truly honor ourselves and one another?

I'll finish this section by coming back to something I've mentioned earlier since it's extremely essential: **ANYTHING that stops you from fulfilling your greatest human potential and your Life's highest purpose and distracts you from your commitment to yourSelf can be considered toxic.**

It is imperative you become very clear as to what does or doesn't align with that commitment. It's a step by step process and it will keep on changing since you are constantly changing as well. The one thing that remains the same, is your commitment to yourSelf. The more you develop your skills of discernment and the ability to follow your own compass, the stronger your foundation will be.

Try this one out:

This is something I like to do with those I work with and in my own Life. It helps to get clearer on your goals, your commitments, and the actions that will assist you on your chosen path. Of course, you can use this contract for any purpose – this is between you and yourSelf, so make it your own by changing it or adding things you see fit.

YOUR SPECIAL CONTRACT WITH YOURSELF

This is a tool to help you stay committed to taking empowering steps and to stay committed to your desired vision. The key to growing and expanding your awareness and to serving Life in a greater way is to commit to taking little right actions. I invite you to sign this sacred contract and commit to what you promise yourSelf.

To _____ (your name)

As of today, I commit to follow my personal guidance system at
all times. What are two things I KNOW I am guided to do in my
Life right now, and so I must follow?

1: _____

_____

_____

_____

2: _____

_____

_____

_____

What in my Life HELPS me stay on course? (personal habits,
belief systems, relationships, activities, etc.)_____

_____

_____

_____

_____

What in my Life KNOCKS me off course? (personal habits, belief
systems, relationships, activities, etc.)_____

_____

_____

_____

_____

As of today, I choose to start using more discernment in my Life and allow in **only** that which helps me stay on course, enhances the quality of my Life, and supports me in achieving my goals for mySelf. In following this choice, I commit to take these two action steps:

Action step #1: _____

_____

_____

Action step #2: _____

_____

_____

As of today, I commit to establish healthy personal boundaries that support my commitment to mySelf and my well-being. This commitment will result in: _____

_____

_____

_____

As of today, I commit to this new belief about mySelf: I believe that I AM..._____

_____

_____

_____

I am committed to these goals because I am committed to having the BEST and most fulfilling relationship with mySelf! I believe in my process and I know that taking all these small right actions consistently will greatly enhance my Life and the Life of others.

Signed_____Date _____

Building Block #4: Give yourSelf some f#*%ing credit

Let's face it. How often do we give ourselves credit? And I'm not talking about giving yourSelf credit for things you accomplish in Life, (which is great of course), I'm talking about giving yourSelf credit for just being alive, for being human. For being YOU. Do you realize what it takes to be a human being? Do you recognize your own uniqueness? When was the last time you looked at yourSelf in the mirror and acknowledged your beauty, your brilliance, and your miraculous nature? When was the last time you took a moment to appreciate who you are and all that you do, even that which seems to be "insignificant"? When was the last time you gave yourSelf a juicy compliment? Or don't you think you deserve any compliments and credit until you "prove" to be worthy? Why are we being so stingy with ourselves?? Let's take care of that, shall we?

As I shared with you earlier, my own inner judge used to be my worst enemy; and I know I'm not the only one. It took me years to shift from being my worst enemy to being my best enemy, to being my friend, my good friend, my best friend, my closest friend, my most loving friend, companion, lover, parent and biggest fan of all; a work in progress still, for sure.

But learning how to compliment mySelf (for everything) and give mySelf credit for just being alive has been one of the most pivotal, Life changing skills I could have ever added to my tool box; which requires a complete shift in perception.

Perceiving yourSelf as a masterpiece worthy to be acknowledged for will establish a new foundation in your Life. To build this foundation, start giving yourSelf words of appreciation **every single day.** When we have a more rounded and complete perception of what it means to be alive, we learn that each of us as a human being is so much more than just flesh and bones acting up a certain character – *who you are is not a random thing and you specifically chose to be you at this moment in time*

You might say that you don't remember choosing any of this, so what the hell am I talking about? Well, do you remember our car analogy? Your physical body being the vehicle and your soul being the engine under the hood? Your soul is the driving, Life-giving force of the vehicle that is you; it was your soul who chose the Life you are experiencing right now. It was your soul who chose to be who you are, in the body that you inhabit, with your unique mind, your unique dreams, the journey you are on, the Life circumstances you encounter, the highs, the lows, the lessons, the triumphs, the twists and the turns. It was your soul who decided to be the engine for your vehicle so you could go on this particular road trip of your Life's journey.

I ask you to close your eyes for a moment and take a deep breath… Feel into who you are as a soul. You don't need to know what a soul is or even believe in it. Just let yourSelf feel that force operating within you. Let yourSelf feel that engine under the hood of your human vehicle. Your soul is as unique as you are so your experience of it is unique to you. You need to feel it for yourSelf... connect to it in your own way. It might just be a feeling or a sensation, maybe a deep sense of knowing. It might have a color or a shape, and it might feel like something familiar; similarly to what feels like HOME.

And what does your soul have anything to do with giving yourSelf some credit? It as EVERYTHING to do with it! When we don't acknowledge that aspect of ourselves, it is easy to slip into a shallow viewing of who we are; the belief that you are nothing more than an insignificant person just doing his or her thing. That shallow viewpoint is an open door for Self judgment and a lack of appreciation for who you **truly** are and what it takes to be you. Let's pause here and do a quick Life review – from the moment you can remember yourSelf being alive until now:

Everything you have lived through.

Every step and milestone.

Every heartbreak.

Every challenge.

Every breakdown.

Every breakthrough.

Every triumph.

Every lesson.

Every change.

Every accomplishment, no matter how small.

Every time you have fallen down and gotten back up.

Every time you have fallen down and didn't get back up.

The good days.

The bad days.

The in between days.

The highs and the lows.

Moments of joy and moments of despair.

Moments of Love and moments of loss.

Moments of celebration and moments of pain.

Moments of laughter and moments of tears.

Times of creation and times of destruction.

Times of clarity and times of confusion.

Times of peace and times of complete chaos.

All of the choices you've made along the way that brought you to this moment in time...

Do you still think you don't deserve any credit? Not even a little bit?

We can no longer live under the impression that who we are is nothing more than a breathing, moving machine in a meat suit. How meaningless is that? It feels so uninteresting and mundane. That kind of perception is exactly why the majority of people don't treat themselves as a living miracle. We celebrate ourselves once a year (thank god for birthdays) when in fact, we deserve to be celebrated *every single day*. It doesn't mean you need to throw yourSelf a party every day (which by all means, do it if you feel inspired), it just means that once you realize what it takes to be a human being and how special you are, nothing about you and your Life will ever seem mundane ever again. Even what you consider mundane will become miraculous and you'll start giving yourSelf credit for it.

To be able to implement this building block on a regular basis, it is essential you see yourSelf through this expanded lense. If all you perceive is an image of a person with a bunch of flaws and to-do lists, giving yourSelf credit and appreciating yourSelf would be quite difficult. The more you widen your perception of yourSelf, the more you'll be able to authentically appreciate yourSelf on a consistent basis which will only boost up your Self-worth, your confidence, and your courage to grab Life by the horns. It will strengthen your relationship with yourSelf and will fill up your cup to the max. So no more being stingy with yourSelf!

I would like to offer you a simple way in which you can start widening your perception of yourSelf and your Self-worth. It is called the art of accepting and receiving compliments. I call it art because it does take practice. The majority of us weren't taught to do this, so we are here to start our own new training. You might go through a phase of "fake it till you make it", but don't let that discourage you. All is required is taking the first step which is becoming aware of something you do habitually and perhaps have been doing your whole Life. The shift will occur naturally as you start becoming more comfortable with receiving compliments – whether these compliments are given to you by others or yourSelf.

Try this one on:

The Art of accepting and receiving compliments

SO many people have a hard time with this one. I know I had to overcome this hurdle and at times, I still find mySelf uncomfortable when being showered with compliments. It's crazy. Whoever came up with the plan of keeping us in a small and tight container of Self-criticism and judgment did a great job. But we are here to say *no more*. The tides are shifting...

Right now, let's make a deal to fully accept compliments as you would a gift. Sincere compliments are just that. Gifts. Energetic gifts. There is absolutely no sane reason why we would reject the gift of a kind word or a juicy compliment but some of us find ways to argue against them, even giving reasons why they aren't true. More often than not, I encounter people's shocked reaction when I compliment them for their awesomeness with no "apparent reason". I either get 'Why, what did I do?' or 'Why are you saying that'? We've been trained to actually doubt compliments we receive or assume we need to do something before we can be deserving of an acknowledgment.

Just to add to that, misplaced modesty can actually ruin a moment of joyful exchange with another person. Rejecting someone's kind words is like rejecting a gift they are giving you. Feels kinda shitty, wouldn't you say? We can easily accept a compliment with humility by simply saying "Thank you." It might feel uncomfortable at first but I encourage you to resist the urge to reject a compliment next time it is being offered to you. **You must train yourSelf to know that you are valued and worthy of being acknowledged.** At the end of the day, the person complimenting you is only stating the obvious. So accept the gift and shut up.

If it's lack of Self-esteem or overbearing inner critic that is responsible for your inability to accept a compliment, the first step would be to start believing good things about yourSelf. How do you do that? One of my favorite things to do (wasn't at first, believe me), is giving mySelf compliments in the mirror. You will feel silly initially, big time, you might even feel stuck – but over time it will start to feel more natural and you'll notice just how good it feels; you might even start liking it…

Start putting yourSelf and who you are on your gratitude list, remembering just what it takes to be a human being… what it means to be you. Start feeling good about celebrating yourSelf because **this world could use more individuals who truly know who they are and are not afraid to celebrate that**. This is paving a way for society and humanity to start celebrating one another and Life as a whole. Again (and I'll keep on hammering this one), there's nothing selfish or narcissistic in celebrating and appreciating yourSelf.

On that note, I also invite you to start giving compliments to others. Just for fun. It can be a good friend or the cashier at the store. Make this a frequent practice – speaking kind words of appreciation to other people. By reminding others of their greatness and beauty you will not only lift their spirit up but you'll also notice how great it feels to make another person feel appreciated and seen. If they doubt your words or 'reject' your compliment (because they too are conditioned to do so), notice how different it feels when the gift you offer is not received. After you experience both sides, you will be ready to play along more fully, acknowledging the value of your appreciative words to yourSelf and others.

Building Block #5: The Fun Factor –
Don't take any of this too seriously

I'm intentionally closing this section with this building block because things can feel a bit heavy or serious when we talk about all this stuff. Well, I have learned that without humor, fun, laughter, pleasure, play, and the ability to lighten up that which can feel heavy, you don't stand a chance on this Life journey. Mastering your Life sounds like serious business (and I definitely take it very seriously), yet at the same time we must balance out the seriousness of it all with a lighter approach; it's the never-ending dichotomy of Life – this is all very serious and at the same time it's really not.

A sense of lightness and fun is crucial to your well-being. Without it, we can very easily feel weighed down by the immensity of what it takes to be a human being who is choosing to upgrade their Life by making a lifelong commitment to themselves. Mastery (of any kind) is a state of recalibration – a constant unfolding of your highest and greatest potential as a human being. When we get stuck on the idea that we need to perfect ourselves, our journey goes from enjoyable to burdensome; which feels like heavy weight. We can get too caught up in all of this serious business while forgetting the most important thing: *We are here to in-joy ourselves and to have fun on our Life's adventure.*

One of the ways in which you can lighten up the load for yourSelf and have more fun with all of this is by learning how to laugh **with** yourSelf. It is a simple yet very profound shift of attitude. Once we break the barriers of Self-judgment, Self-criticism, and over the top Self-perfectionism (by treating yourSelf like a precious child), we gain so much more internal freedom which allows us to approach our Life's journey in a lighter way – replacing our harsh judgments with some good jokes (yes, at our own expense).

For example, now days, every time an old pattern creeps back in or when I make a silly move of any kind, I just let mySelf be entertained by the whole thing. Like I've mentioned earlier, talking to mySelf out loud is one of the ways in which I make light of whatever it is I'm going through at any particular moment. I choose a lighter approach with whatever arises within me and around me. Because let's admit it, we sometimes act so ridiculously it's impossible not to laugh! I'm not suggesting you laugh at other people (that's their choice to do or not), I'm just suggesting you learn how to zoom out a bit and acknowledge all the ways in which your behaviour does indeed deserve a good laugh every once in awhile. Beside, laughter has been proven to improve our well-being, so why not utilize every chance we get?

As with any other relationships, when the fun factor is missing, the relationship suffers; same thing applies to your relationship with yourSelf. Whatever tools and practices you find in this book that speak to you, take it and have fun with it. Even though the initial stages might not feel fun at all, just aim for that. You'll be very surprised to discover how quickly your attitude can shift when you approach yourSelf (and Life) from a place of Love rather than judgment and with a clear intention to in-joy your journey rather than to struggle with it.

Having more fun on this journey also means that you make space in your Life to do things just for fun; things that bring you pure pleasure and joy. So many people feel guilty for this, or they think it's a waste of time. The truth is, making space in your Life to **just have fun** is actually an act of Self-Love. Releasing any guilt around your play and leisure time is directly related to your sense of Self-worth. Your play time is food for your heart and soul. It's nourishment for your inner child. It's fuel for all the other things you have on your to-do list.

Find a happy balance between your to-do list and your play time but both must be included. If you are challenged with this idea and find it hard to create time in your schedule for fun and play, know that it will naturally shift the more you develop your Self-worth and Love for yourSelf. If this is not something that comes naturally to you, if you struggle to find time for your play, you can start by putting fun activities on your schedule (you know, start taking your fun seriously). You might just start with once a week. That's fine. Even if it's only 15 minutes of doing something *just for fun*. No agenda, no goal, nothing to accomplish except the sheer pleasure of having fun, like a little child. I invite you to do that for a while and see if you still believe that your play time is in fact a wasted time.

Your idea of what fun is, what you consider to be your play time is something changeable. As you change internally, what brings you pleasure will change accordingly so just be aware of that and keep following what feels like true fun for you. Old habits and preferences will find their way out of your Life as you continue to discover a new relationship with yourSelf and master your Life in a new way.

Another way you can bring more lightness and joy into your everyday Life is by sprinkling little bits of fun even on the most tedious and "un-fun" activities. Before you're about to tackle your to-do list, ask yourSelf: ***How can I make this more fun for mySelf?*** The answer will differ depending on the task at hand but no matter how you choose to bring more playfulness and fun into your daily Life, it will be a game changer. Get creative with your taxes, with your bills, with your work, with cleaning the toilet, with going to the bank or the store. You'll be amazed how a tedious task can turn into something quite enjoyable only by shifting your perception of it.

Play your favorite music while scrubbing the toilet and sing like nobody's listening...

Wear a funny costume while filing your taxes or paying your bills and pretend to be a financial super hero...

Strike a few dance moves while waiting in line at the bank or the grocery store...

Imagination and creativity are fun's best allies so don't be afraid to use them. Why do you think children are so joyful and light? They let their imagination run free. And as you know, that child-like version of yourSelf still lives within you so give yourSelf the permission to have more fun with him or her. Let your imagination and creativity become active participants in your Life as often and as much as possible. We can be responsible and mature adults and still know how to play and have fun like little children. We can be committed and dedicated to our Life's journey while not taking ourselves or any of this too seriously. We can be sensitive and sincere and still be able to have a good sense of humor with it all.

See your Life as your playground. As serious as Self-Mastery might sound, it is meant to be enjoyable; your human experience is meant to be enjoyable. Lighten your load by adopting a lighter approach, an open mind, and a lighter heart who's eager to laugh and Love as much as possible. **You deserve every ounce of that joyful Love.**

Chapter 5

WHY does it matter

"The very Well-Being of the planet depends on the way you handle your body, your feelings, Your Perceptions and your Consciousness." - *Thich Nhat Hanh*

I am choosing to start this chapter with an extremely prevalent and unfortunate misconception, one that runs deep within our social construct: Loving yourSelf means you're either Self-absorbed, selfish, or the best one of all – narcissist. I've heard it all. We've been fed so much crap by those who would prefer humans to stay in their own little holes of Self-deprecation, Self-limitations and distorted sense of personal power. It is borderline insane. Being humble is a wonderful quality and something I aspire to live by every single day however, humble doesn't mean you don't Love, appreciate, and celebrate who you are and your divine nature.

The definition of humility is: *Freedom from pride or arrogance; the quality or state of being humble.* To me, being humble simply means to know my own innate magnificence (as part of this exquisite creation) **while** acknowledging I am merely the conduit, the vehicle that carries this powerful and mysterious Life force (which makes taking care of this vehicle even that much more important)! **Loving yourSelf and having the audacity to announce to the world that you are a piece of art doesn't need to come with arrogance.** Let's not confuse arrogance with confidence and complete lack of Self-esteem with humility. There's a healthy way to express your Love and appreciation for yourSelf without getting lost in yourSelf – that's part of your Self-Mastery. Humanity at large will only benefit from more individuals who are indeed confidant, know their divine nature, use their innate gifts wisely, and do all of that with humility.

So loving yourSelf doesn't make you less humble or turns you into a narcissist. The definition of Narcissism is: *Excessive interest in or admiration of oneSelf and one's physical appearance; Extreme Selfishness, with a grandiose view of one's own talents and a craving for admiration;* Can you truly Love yourSelf and be a narcissist? Not so much. Those we describe as narcissists are usually the ones who don't *really* Love themselves because they constantly seek admiration from others so they can validate their own worth. They wear a mask of Self-importance to cover up a deep lack of confidence. Those are people who need to put others down or below them to feel powerful and important. It may seem as though they Love themselves, but that's only a clever cover up. They may be in Love with their power, but not with themselves because they don't even know who they truly are.

When a person truly Loves themSelves, the last thing they need is other people's validation so they can feel important or seen, and they're most certainly not interested in treating anyone poorly; as a narcissist would.

Putting yourSelf first doesn't make you selfish either. I'm baffled by the fact that so many people have their list of priorities upside down where their well-being and needs (sometimes even the most basic needs), are at the very bottom of the list; everything and everyone comes before them. We live with this unfortunate misconception that service and acts of Love have to look like extreme Self-sacrifice and over-giving. But we must find our way out of this perception and recognize that **a full Life that is dedicated to serving others doesn't mean we toss our own well-being to the nearest trashcan.** To be of best service, whether it's your family, your marriage, your partnership, your job, your clients, your community, your church or whatever is your way of giving back, you must be taken care of first. If you don't put the oxygen mask on yourSelf first, you'll run out of juice very quickly. How many times have you faced the same burned-out feeling? That's your own Self telling you to pay attention.

So pay attention. Put Self-Love into action, release any feelings of guilt you may be carrying around it and start filling up your cup until it overflows – when your Love is overflowing, when you are nourished and fulfilled on all levels, everyone benefits from it and one by one, we are creating a new foundation for humanity and this world at large.

"Self-Love is an ocean and your heart is a vessel. Make it full, and any excess will spill over into the lives of the people you hold dear. But you MUST come first."- *Beau Taplin*

It is important to really understand this concept and see the bigger picture – to see that because we are all so interconnected, loving yourSelf and mastering your Life has a tremendous impact on not just your Life but on everything and everyone you come in contact with. As Thich Nhat Hanh writes, the well-being of humanity and our planet is actually *dependent* on how each and every one of us CHOOSES to handle ourselves – body, mind, heart, and soul.

As humans, we've been given a few very important powers, one of them is the power of choice. Since every great power comes with great responsibility, the power of choice, when put into the hands of humans, can become either a blessing or a curse. It all depends on our level of awareness and mindfulness – our ability to acknowledge the greater impact our choices have. The question which arises from here is how do we use this power we've been so graciously gifted with?

One of my yoga teachers used to say: ***The way you do anything is the way you do everything.*** This statement has really stuck with me. When observing Life and our choices with that in mind, we realize how brutally true this statement is; no matter how subtly it may show up. We must zoom out from our limited perspective to fully comprehend the immense value of mastering one's Life; only then can you observe how much of a difference you actually make just by loving yourSelf like you never have before.

Consider the different situations and choices you face every single day and how you choose to go about them. Some of the choices are minor and some have much bigger implications yet, even the choices that may appear insignificant can have long term effects; both on you personally and on your outer circle. Your personal Life is a part of a much larger picture – it's a part of a web where **everything is connected.** By making better choices that are driven by Love for oneSelf, you make the most positive impact on the entire web. And **when guided by Self-Love, EVERY choice you make will be based on that and that alone.**

As an individual cell in the body of Life, we each occupy our own personal domain. Your personal domain interacts with other domains in the same way cells in the body interact with one another. As we continue to zoom out further and further, we can see that all the individual cells or domains are indeed the building blocks of the entire network. Now, what would make a healthier, stronger, more harmonious, more loving, and more cohesive network? The obvious answer, of course, is healthy, strong, harmonious, loving and cohesive cells. And what brings individual cells to that state? Creating the healthiest, most harmonious and most loving conditions for each cell to thrive in.

As individuals, when our personal domain is comprised of Love, inner joy, fulfillment, harmony, and true well-being, we begin to interact with everything else around us in the same manner. **The inner state and level of well-being of each individual will determine the way that individual interacts with its external world**; quite impactful I would say. The moment one truly knows, loves, and sees oneSelf as a divine masterpiece and nothing less than that, the moment one acknowledges one is not *separate* from Life, but is, in fact *Life itself*, EVERYTHING becomes a sacred ground to be treated with the utmost respect, appreciation, reverence and Love.

So, do you still think that loving yourSelf like never before is just about you?

BE THE CHANGE YOU WISH TO SEE IN THE WORLD

I stand behind this statement of Gandhi wholeheartedly and base all of my teachings on it. I truly don't see any other way. The state of our planet and humanity cannot be improved or elevated if we don't elevate ourselves as individuals – physically, mentally, emotionally, and spiritually; and nothing can elevate us more than our ability to master our Life and to master it with Love. That is the latest and greatest upgrade we can install in our consciousness. This Love software is available for download whenever you choose to click the 'ok' button and start the reprogramming process. The doors of heaven are the doors of your heart believe it or not. It might feel unfamiliar, scary, hard and even painful at times, but it's time to open these doors wide and rise in Love with who you are – all of us will only go higher from there.

Creating heaven on Earth is up to us but we each must find that heaven within us first. With that said, I invite you to ask yourSelf the following question:

What is it I wish to see in the world and how can I create more of that in my Life, starting with mySelf?

Is it more peace?

More Love?

More compassion?

More kindness?

More acceptance?

More ease?

More balance?

More harmony?

More health and well-being?

More mindfulness?

More honesty and integrity?

More freedom?

More cohesiveness?

More joy?

More passion for Life?

I can safely say that all of us would like to see more of the above in our world today. We can all agree that our planet and humanity will thrive more under these conditions. However, if we truly desire to experience real and positive changes in the world, we **must** be that, not just talk about it. Knowing that each one of us is a cell in the larger body of Life becomes a compelling motivating force to embody these qualities.

The state of disharmony and ill-being in the world is the result of a deeper issue. This current state is simply reflecting back to us the malfunctions of humanity as a collective in the same way the human body gets to a state of ill-being or dis-ease as a result of an internal imbalance or malfunction of some sort. Any imbalance, pain, lack of compassion, and lack of Love we see in the world are the symptoms we are experiencing on the surface. But what do we find when we track the root cause of these symptoms? Well, we find wounded, unbalanced, and unaware individuals who are simply needing more harmony in their lives and in one way or another, screaming for attention and Love.

Addressing the root cause of any issue, whether in our personal lives or in the world at large, is the key for **long-lasting and significant changes**. We can no longer continue treating the symptoms while disregarding what caused them in the first place. Knowing the impact our personal choices have on the entire network propels us to make the healthiest, most harmonious choices possible; choices driven by radical Self-Love. By choosing to master your Life, you agree to hold yourSelf fully ac-countable for your personal domain which requires you to address the root cause of **any** symptoms you may experience in your Life. Whether it's physical, emotional, mental, or spiritual discomfort, taking a pill or distracting yourSelf from the discomfort in whichever way will only keep the root cause alive. To experience a true state of harmony and well-being, we must choose to go straight to the source and address it with understanding.

Living in a state of harmony and well-being as an individual automatically translates into living in harmony with others and with the Earth. That's just how it works. A simple cause and effect. You can't start making healthier choices for your Life without having a positive effect on the world around you. You can't become more kind and caring with yourSelf without feeling that for others and for the planet. You can't become more loving with yourSelf without becoming more loving towards everything and everyone else. That's one of the magical powers of rising in Love with yourSelf – it will actually lead you to rise in Love with Life itself.

Now just imagine how the world is going to look like if enough individuals chose to live in this way...

This doesn't mean we don't take action in the world to make a significant difference. Creating solutions to some of the issues we are facing at this time of human history is very important and helpful; it's just not enough. The work we do "out there" has to be backed up by the inner work. Without doing the inner work, any external attempts to change the status quo and the issues in front of us are quite futile. They won't last because they are being implemented onto an unstable structure built on a shaky foundation. As the building blocks of humanity's foundation, **we** are the ones who are responsible for the structure's instability. But we are also the ones who have the power to strengthen it with our loving and mindful choices.

The implications of deeply loving yourSelf and learning how to master your Life are so large and wide. The ripple effects of both functions are infinite and will be felt by many generations to come. The days of being called selfish for loving yourSelf are over as we are creating a new foundation for a healthier, happier, more loving, and more elevated humanity. Love will become a universal religion where every individual is a devotee – dedicated to oneSelf and to Life as a whole. When Love is our guiding light, everything else falls away. Mastering your Life and your relationship with yourSelf will create a space for you to to live so fully and presently in Love that there will be no room for anything else to exist.

Now zoom out… From your own personal domain onto the entire network. An entire network that lives *so fully and presently in Love that there's no room for anything else to exist.* How does that sound?

I hope some day you'll join us and the world will be as one…

Chapter 6

Find God by Finding YourSelf

THE GREAT RECONNECTION

"Recognize that everything in our world is sacred, including us, and that our job is to foster the fullest expression of that divinity." - *Alberto Villoldo, Ph.D.*

As I mentioned at the beginning of the book, God, to me, is Life. All of Life. It's not someone or something that lives somewhere in the sky looking at us through a magnifying glass, and we are certainly not separate from that source we refer to as God. Human beings are either taught to believe that God is an image outside of themselves to be worshiped and feared by or the complete opposite, which is not believing in anything that we can't see, rationalize and quantify. Yet, if we realize that God is not a localized image or a thing, but is actually everything and is everywhere, our idea of God changes.

Your spiritual journey is to find what God is to you based on your own exploration and inner truth rather than believing in religious concepts or other people's beliefs. Most importantly, you must acknowledge your own godly existence; because if **everything** is God, you are not exempt from that whole. It is crucial we learn how to close the gap between that which we call God and that which we call human. In other words, *you don't need to look very far to find God – just look in the mirror.*

I never had a strong belief about God one way or another, but I most certainly didn't dare to include mySelf in the same category as God. There were these questions, though, that always kept echoing in the back of my mind: *What is the meaning of Life, anyway? Why am I here and who am I?* These questions usually propel us in the direction of our spiritual exploration. Knowingly or not, with the intention to find God or not, it is our soul nudging us in the direction of the great re-connection – to God, yes, but through the great re-connection to oneSelf first.

What if the meaning of Life was as simple as getting to know yourSelf as Life's masterpiece? As God in physical form? To Love yourSelf so fully and deeply and see that God lives inside of you? inside of everyone and everything else? What if the reason for your existence was for you to see yourSelf in the eyes of God – full of Love and compassion rather than harsh and judgmental? **What if the meaning of Life was to just wake up to your own divinity and know God by truly knowing who you are?**

Wanting to know God and the meaning of Life while being blind to the fact that you are indeed a living miracle is like ignoring a big unicorn sitting in the middle of your living room calling out your name. We've learned to disregard the most obvious thing of all while searching and reaching for answers in all the wrong places. Who you are, a human being, is such a supreme creation, a living, breathing miracle who deserves to be treated as such. If we keep disregarding that fact, we're really missing the point. How in the world can we fully be connected to God (Life) if our connection to ourselves is completely distorted?

How would your Life look like if you started looking for God and Life's meaning inside yourSelf rather than outside? If you actually admired yourSelf as a whole package? That's not to say there aren't external fulfillments which add to the meaning of Life; after all, God is everything and everywhere so every task, every job, every gesture, every relationship, every connection to another living being helps us get more in touch with the richness of Life – the richness that is God. But you must include yourSelf in that rich display of awesomeness.

And why is it so important, you might ask? What does God have anything to do with mastering your Life? Well, it has everything to do with it. As we know, Life can be challenging – full of twists and turns and many different things pulling on us all at the same time. We have a physical body to care for, different emotions and thoughts for us to manage, earthly responsibilities we must attend to, goals and aspirations we want to fulfill… the list continues on and on. When we don't have a strong spiritual foundation, we can very easily get pulled by the strong currents of Life. We can get buried underneath it all and feel suffocated at times.

Do you remember the analogy of your ego looking at Life from inside the valley while your soul is standing at the top of the mountain? Your soul is the part in you that is connected to what I call God; the same part that can see the bigger picture of Life, rather than just the nitty gritty details of reality (which by the way, are not less Godly, you just don't want to get too caught up in that). Your soul is the invincible part of you – the Godly power you hold. In order to handle all of the different layers of your Life and master it in the process, having a strong connection to this invincible source is not only needed, it is crucial; to see that God is a powerful Life force that lives in everything and to know that it lives in you as well. That knowing gives you the ability to stand on the mountain top and see Life from a bird's eye view on a **consistent basis.**

To attain that expanded point of view, you must believe in something greater than what your ego or mind can logically comprehend; to see yourSelf as more than just your personality. Call it God or call it whatever you want, at the end of the day, we need that strong line of connection to live a Life of mastery that is rich and full of wisdom. And that line of connection begins by knowing yourSelf – ALL of yourSelf. And then loving yourSelf – ALL of yourSelf. As a child of God and part of Life's greater masterpiece, it's the least you can do.

THE DIVINE PLAN
We must have FAITH

Our connection to that which we call God has to include a healthy dose of Faith – a massive amount of Faith, actually. Our Faith is an essential part of our spiritual foundation and a necessary force you want to cultivate within you. By Faith, I don't mean religion. Faith has nothing to do with religion. It's quite absurd to see humans fighting each other in the name of religion; in the name of God. If we look at the fundamentals of every single religion, they all say the exact same thing. They may have different names to describe God but they are all based on Faith – Faith in God.

If we perceive God to be the orchestrating force of this entire creation rather than a single thing or a specific image, we discover that our Faith in God is basically Faith in Life itself. The interconnectivity in which we live helps us remember that each of us is indeed a part of this perfectly designed web with an immense intelligence behind it – from the air in our lungs to the wind outside; from the blood in our veins to the running rivers; from the tears we shed to the rain falling from the sky; from the water we drink to the waves in the ocean; from our heart beating in our chest to the sun rising and setting each day...

Do you ever doubt whether the sun is going to rise in the morning? Even on a cloudy day, you know the sun is there; you may not see it (maybe not even for days), but you don't question whether it's there or not. You just *know*. Well, my friend, that's what true Faith is all about – a deep sense of knowing that all is well. Even when you can't see all the details or the light at the end of the tunnel, (just like when the sun is hidden behind the clouds), you still know all is working out perfectly. It might not always be your plan but rest assured, there's a bigger picture you can't always see – A Divine Plan.

On the journey of Self-Mastery, we gradually start aligning our ego based personality with our soul. From an ego perspective (which is attached to certain outcomes and desires) or from our mind's point of view (which likes to analyse and worry), there's nothing scarier than a mysterious plan which cannot be known ahead of time or be explained in a rational manner. However, having a strong connection with your soul makes it easier to trust the divine plan even though you might not know what's in store for you.

By developing your strong Faith, you begin to live with an unwavering knowing that no matter what happens in Life, no matter how things appear to be on the surface, Life/God **always** supports your highest good. And that is very helpful, to say the least. It is your Faith which makes you resilient. It opens your mind to see that anything is possible. It helps you believe not only in God but more importantly, in yourSelf. Your Faith is the bridge between the known and the unknown, the source from which you are able to draw courage, will, and confidence to follow your heart's desires, your biggest dreams, and your intuition; especially when none of it makes much sense. Without Faith, we are not able to leave our comfort zone and believe that maybe, just maybe, Life has something much greater in store for us than all of our plans combined.

Fulfilling our greatest potential as human beings requires us to expand and that expansion sometimes asks us to take a leap of Faith. Leaps of Faith are those moments in Life we choose to take a bold step and skip from point A to point B without seeing point B in our view – we can't see it but we KNOW it's there… we don't know what's there but we do it anyway because taking that step feels so right. Courage is not the absence of fear – it's feeling the fear and choosing to do it anyway; whatever the 'it' may be. The only way we can choose to take that leap despite our fears is knowing and believing in ourselves and in God, utilizing our Faith as an antidote to our fears.

Every time I've ever taken a leap of Faith in my Life, every time I've jumped off a cliff into an unknown territory (metaphorically speaking, of course… please don't go jumping off any cliffs), my Life unfolded in the most incredible ways. Now, looking back, I recognize that those leaps were orchestrated by my soul's wisdom, driven by a much greater plan than I was aware of.

One of the biggest leaps I've taken on my journey thus far was leaving Israel at the age of 20. I was bored and heart broken at the time, feeling like I had to change my reality; there was a strong urge inside of me demanding a radical shift. I was faced with a choice: to stay where I was, feeling miserable and blaming Life for what was going on **or** to take a different turn and let Life lead me somewhere else. I chose the latter. Without Faith, which gave me the courage to listen and follow the guidance of my soul, I wouldn't have taken that leap. No way. But I did. I took that leap because the pain of staying in my comfort zone (which was very uncomfortable, anyway) was far greater than the fear of the unknown. And so, fully backed up by my Faith, I followed the urge.

From the moment I made the choice to leave, it took me exactly one month until I was on my way to New York City. I had one friend in the city, absolutely no plan and certainly no idea that this 6 to 12 month trip would turn out to be a lot more than just a trip. Never in my wildest dreams (and definitely not according to any logical plan), could I have ever predicted that this one leap of Faith would turn into the grand adventure I've been on for the last 14 years since I left Israel (and still counting). That's how the divine plan works – you don't need to know (and you'll never know) all that is awaiting your arrival. All you need to do is follow what you feel guided to do in the moment; no matter how irrational or frightening it may seem. A much better Life is available for you when you realize that the future offers you infinite possibilities and not only one road.

When you start deepening your relationship with yourSelf, you'll begin to notice the different urges that arise within you. These urges will nudge you to change your reality in some way, make a move, take a step in a new direction or explore something completely new and unknown. It's not enough to only notice these urges – we must act upon that which we feel guided to do; sometimes it's easy, but sometimes it can be very scary. That's when your Faith in God's divine plan comes in. The first step is making choices that reflect your sense of Self-worth and Love for yourSelf and then it is your Faith and connection to God that give you the courage to act, especially when it comes to those tough decisions or big leaps.

As the years go by, my relationship with mySelf deepens, and I become more connected to my true Self by aligning my ego with the wisdom of my soul. The more I connect to my true Self, the more I deepen my relationship and my connection to God; to the divine intelligence of Life. My unwavering Faith keeps getting stronger and stronger, which is definitely my anchor and my saving grace during moments of challenge and doubt. It's what keeps my head above water when the ocean of Life gets stormy or rough. Mastering our lives doesn't make us immune to Life's challenges or growing pains, it merely places us in a more empowered position to face the challenges and to approach our pain with compassion while knowing it is truly a gift. And that takes Faith. Plenty of it.

As part of your spiritual exploration, I invite you to review the following:

- **How do you see the image of yourSelf as a soul?** Who are you beyond your persona and the different roles you play in Life? How in touch are you with that part of yourSelf and what can you do to strengthen that line of communication? This exploration will require you to start noticing where are the gaps in your Life; the ways in which you need to let your ego and mind catch up with the wisdom of your soul and the voice of guidance within you.
- **Who and what is God in your Life?** What is the quality of your Faith

– Faith In God, in Life, and in yourSelf? How strong is your connection to this great force and what can you do to strengthen that connection?

Your spiritual foundation is an absolute must on your Life's journey and an essential element that will enrich your Life in a profound way. In the second part of the book, I will share spiritual tools and practices that will assist you in establishing a clearer and stronger connection with your soul and with God. Establishing this connection becomes vital when we tackle the most critical question of all: **Why are you here?**

YOUR SPECIFIC ROLE AND PURPOSE

We can get lost in the idea that our purpose, or role in Life, is only determined by what it is we do or choose to be in the world. That's an incomplete approach. It is the reason why so many individuals who do utilize their talents and skills and accomplish a lot in the world still feel a sense of emptiness. That sense of emptiness is the soul craving to be recognized and loved by them, calling them to rise in Love with themselves and wake up to their divine nature; which is so much more than just a persona or the roles we play. Yes, we each carry our own unique signature, a unique blueprint, a specific instrument we are here to play. There's something for each of us to contribute to the larger symphony of Life, but it doesn't end there.

In the context of the divine plan and our specific role in it, let's look at Life as a big orchestra playing a symphony. There are many different instruments all playing together with one conductor whose job is to orchestrate the entire thing. Each instrument has a distinct role and a specific way in which it contributes to the overall sound of the symphony. The only thing each player is responsible for is focusing on their own instrument and the part they need to play while paying close attention to the cues of the conductor. And while each player with their instrument adds a specific sound to the totality of the symphony, they all share *one mutual purpose* – creating the most beautiful music together. They also know that in order to achieve that, *each must fine tune and master their own individual instrument as best they can.*

Within this big Life symphony, the conductor is the vital force who orchestrates all of Life (call it God) and each of us is a player in the orchestra. The player represents who you are as a persona while the instrument represents your soul. Your persona and your soul need one another in order to create music; in order to translate the notes from the page into an actual sound. However, in order to create **harmonious sound**, the player must get close with their instrument, learn how to play it, and eventually how to master it. The player must get familiar with all the different notes, octaves, ranges, and capabilities of their instrument. In essence, the player must become ONE with their instrument.

This is the first half of your divine purpose. Similarly to the different players in an orchestra, we too, have one purpose in common in conjunction with our unique individual role. Each player knows that the more they can become one with their instrument, the greater the symphony will be; and so that becomes their purpose – to know their instrument inside and out, connect with it, master it and above all else, Love it. When each of the players plays at that level of attunement, mastery, and devotion, the entire symphony goes to the next level.

When it comes to you and I and every other human on the planet, the one purpose we all have in common is **to become one with our soul;** to become one with our instrument and learn how to play it to the best of our ability. To create the most beautiful melodies possible by getting real close and intimate with our unique instrument; with our unique soul. But in order to do that, you must realize your exquisite nature and recognize that you are indeed a magnificent instrument who deserves to be played with devotion and reverence, with the utmost respect and adoration. And when that merge happens, when you become one with your own instrument, devoted and masterfully in Love, you won't be able to distinguish if it's you playing the instrument or if, in fact, it is the instrument playing you.

Rest assured that by creating the most dedicated and loving relationship with yourSelf, you are not only fulfilling a big part of your purpose here, but you also contribute to the entire fabric of reality as a whole. There will always be a level of restlessness within you if you don't submit yourSelf to your soul in this way. Your soul, being God's spokesperson within you, wants you to see yourSelf in the way God sees you; the way Life sees you – absolutely magnificent and divine. It wants each and every one of us to learn how to Love ourselves unconditionally and treat ourselves as the sacred masterpiece each of us is. It wants every human being to become their own living temple where worship takes place each and every day and with every single breath. **It is not until you are able to look into your eyes and recognize your divinity with complete Love in your heart that your Life purpose is fully fulfilled.**

So with the first half of your purpose in mind, let's move into the second half of the specific role you came here to play as part of the divine plan. That part is your unique blueprint in the same way each instrument has it's own unique sound; and a big part of your purpose is to get in touch with it. The deeper meaning and purpose of your existence goes way beyond what you perceive yourSelf to be or what your ego thinks you need to do and accomplish in order to be fulfilled. All of that is great, but if it's not aligned with your soul's divine plan for you, Life will find a way to redirect you. More often than not, the redirection in your Life shows up as different circumstances, situations, and events and usually those experiences are either uncomfortable, unpredictable, challenging, painful or all of the above. The more you ignore, resist or fight it, the more painful it's going to be.

That was the drive for me when I decided to pick up everything and leave my home country. Even though on the surface everything seemed "perfect" – I had a loving family, lots of friends, a good income, and a "good plan" for the future, I felt a lack of true fulfillment and happiness inside of me. All those friendships I had in my Life started feeling quite unsatisfying; I didn't resonate with them anymore. My relationship with my mom (who I was living with at the time), started going sour, causing me to feel very uncomfortable in my own home. On top of that, I was extremely heart broken because my boyfriend back then ended our relationship, causing me to question my true desires in Life. The overall feeling I had was one of wanting to break free; like everything was going wrong and I was trapped in the twilight zone of my Life.

That burning desire to break free was my soul's way of pointing me in a new direction. I will forever be thankful I was able to listen to the signs Life was giving me at that time. Whether it be external circumstances or the urges we feel within us (and usually the two happen simultaneously), it is our soul communicating with us on the behalf of Life's divine plan – and that communication is not to be ignored.

On your Life's journey, your soul is constantly working within you to help you remember the original promise you made with God; an agreement to carry out a specific set of skills and to accomplish a predetermined mission during your Life on Earth. Your soul diligently keeps on moving you in the direction of fulfilling your role in the divine plan while working on aligning your persona with its divine intelligence. How and if you allow that to occur is up to your own free will, *but understanding that promise and mission is the key factor in determining your true happiness, deep fulfillment, and overflowing abundance.*

Go back and re-read that as many times as you need to, because this understanding will transform you on the deepest levels. You are special. You are unique. You chose to come here to do something that only you can do, something that you and God agreed to together. If your "Life's plan" isn't in accordance with that original agreement, well, things are going to get very uncomfortable. But when you conjure the courage to submit yourSelf to the divine plan using your Faith and your connection to God, you'll not only start remembering who you truly are and what you came here for, you'll be able to move mountains with this inner knowing. And when you combine that inner knowing with a sense of deep Love and devotion – to yourSelf, to God, and to Life (do you see how it's all the same thing?), a true master is born.

Notice what it is you are passionate about in Life. What ignites your fire? What fills your heart with joy and makes you feel at home? What are the things you absolutely Love doing, the things that bring you the most fulfillment? Where do you feel like you are utilizing your skill set and your innate talents in a way that helps you grow while contributing to the larger picture of Life? What is the best way for you to use your unique instrument and which symphony is suitable for you? What urges are alive within you and what is stopping you for responding to them?

All of the above are clues to the role you came here to play – the original agreement you made with God. Following this agreement while cultivating the most loving relationship with yourSelf, will give you a more rounded and meaningful answer to the question – *why am I here*. It will provide you with a deeper understanding of your human experience. I can only share my personal journey of exploration but I can't give you answers to those questions. At the end of the day, it is up to you to discover the answers for yourSelf by getting really close and intimate with your soul as you learn how to master your own instrument. By exploring who you *truly* are, you are arriving home to the God within you to only find yourSelf all over again.

PART TWO

BUILDING THE TEMPLE
OF YOUR LIFE

BECOMING A LIVING TEMPLE

I just Love the word 'temple'. It immediately gives me a sense of reverence, awe and devotion. As you must have learned by now, I refer to temple as a sacred space, a place of worship; but not in a religious way. The worship I'm talking about here is your own human Life and this entire existence as a whole. At the very core, becoming a living temple is what mastering your Life is all about – the ability to make the most out of your physical, mental, emotional and spiritual health and indeed, make Life your temple.

Our ability to do that is dependent on our relationship with ourselves and with God, as I've already described. Our Love for ourselves, when mixed with devotion and reverence for the gift of Life we've been given is the driving force behind our ability to become a living temple – body, mind, heart and soul, all operating as a unified field. As always, we just strive to do our best, taking one step at a time toward unconditional Love, radiant health, and true well-being. It takes time and dedication to master our lives in this way which requires us to be compassionate and gentle with ourselves and most importantly, to really in-joy our temple building process.

Choosing to become a living temple means you need to rectify choices, lifestyle habits, and old conditioning that do not serve you anymore and embrace a new state of being. Allow yourSelf to enter into a new (and perhaps unfamiliar) territory and be open to receive new knowledge that is not available through the mainstream sources. Let the divine intelligence within you guide your way and follow it wholeheartedly. Be diligent with your devotion to the temple of your Life as you continue to move in the direction of your fullest potential, developing habits that bring you into greater alignment with the natural principles of Life.

Within this section, there are practical tools for you to use in order to build your temple. The tools vary from physical, mental, emotional, and spiritual, but it's key to remember that all of those aspects are connected within you – upgrading the health of your body will affect you spiritually and vice versa. In order to build the most stable and luxurious temple possible, you need to focus on each aspect equally. Know which areas in your Life need more attention and strengthening and which areas may already be strong but could use an upgrade.

Becoming a living temple is your Life-long project, so pour your Love and passion into it! Your Life is precious, and you came here to discover just how precious and divine it really is. Make a clear declaration that from this moment forward, your Life will become your temple and Love is your religion. Go out into the world and be a blessing to others by being a living example of true well-being, true joy, radiance, fulfillment, and Love. In-joy your Life to the fullest and celebrate who you are and that which you are becoming.

THE ART OF SIMPLIFYING YOUR LIFE
Why is it so important?

"Be as simple as you can be; you will be astonished to see how uncomplicated and happy your Life can become."
-Paramahansa Yogananda

Becoming a living temple requires us to declutter our inner and outer world. We can't build a temple if there's too much junk laying around. We must clean up the mess first to make room for a new and improved structure; in other words, you want to simplify your Life in every possible way. Just as the quote states, the simpler your Life is (or the simpler you make it to be), the happier and more satisfied you will be. Since we live in a society driven by a 'more is better' attitude, we can get caught up in this mind set and perpetuate a feeling of insatiable hunger; and an endless hunger for more makes things a bit too complicated. **Life is complex, no doubt about it, but it doesn't have to be complicated.** That's why I see it as art – the ability to simplify something extremely complex such as the world we live in.

Confusing simple with boring or not interesting enough is the reason why so many individuals often run away from simple and towards complicated; just to stimulate their system, consciously or not. The feeling of being overstimulated (mentally, emotionally and physically) is an addiction. It is no different than any other drug out there and it works just like any other addiction – if you don't have power over it, it will have power over you. We've been conditioned to overload our system with stimuli almost constantly, confusing the feeling of aliveness with an overstimulated state. This can go on and on very much undetected until we get burned out, sick, exhausted or any other form of what I call ill-being. Do we really need to hit a wall (whatever the wall may be) just so we can learn how to simplify, relax, and slow down?

When driven by Self-Love and well-being, simplifying your inner and outer reality will become second nature. You'll be inspired to do it as a way to keep your temple pure, clean, and vibrant. You'll start noticing that over-stimulating your system causes nothing but stress which is the number one factor for **any** state of ill-being. When you choose to fully commit yourSelf to mastering your Life, your Love for yourSelf will become a bouncer at the door of your temple – anything that is going to damage the temple's interior in any way, is not allowed in; and that is non-negotiable. (Yeah, it's a pretty strict bouncer).

Since the kind of Self-Mastery I'm offering you here is for the purpose of fully participating in the game of Life rather than pulling away from it, the simplicity I'm referring to doesn't imply you sell all of your belongings and move to a cabin in the woods (unless you want to, of course). Although simplifying your possessions is highly recommended (which I'll talk more about), I want to offer you a way to simplify your Life **while** maintaining a rich schedule, if that's your preference. That's why I see it as a form of mastery – the more you learn how to simplify your Life, the more relaxation and peace you'll experience within yourSelf no matter how busy or even chaotic the world around you may seem to be.

It is my intention to make simplicity sexy again, turning our conditioned state of constant hunger (whether it be more stuff, more food, more sex, more drama, more mental, physical, and emotional stimulation) back to our natural state of relaxation where we source our aliveness and zest for Life from within. In this way, simplicity and relaxation don't become boring; they actually become the foundation for what can be a very fulfilling existence minus the extra baggage and drama. Life can truly be simple; we are the ones who insist on making it more complicated than it really is.

I associate simplicity with EASE so that's the feeling I'm asking you to get in touch with as you begin taking inventory. Ease means that there's no struggle within you, no constriction or restriction. Imagine yourSelf trying to take a deep breath while having 200 lbs pressing on your chest... feels pretty dense, heavy and hard, right? That's the energy of complication – it brings with it restriction and lack of ease. Now, remove that weight from your chest and take the deepest breath of your Life... that's what simplicity feels like – The ease that comes from simplifying your reality. There's room to breathe as deep as possible without any unnecessary obstructions. Let that be your baseline.

As we go through the different aspects your temple is made of, you will be asked to reflect on your Life with honesty and acknowledge what can be simplified, adjusted, reorganized or eliminated altogether; in other words, recognize all the extra junk you can no longer store in your temple. As a result of simplifying your personal world, everything else will naturally start moving in that direction, bringing into your Life an amplified sense of ease, relaxation, and well-being.

Chapter 7

The temple of your Body – Your physical well-being

"There is more intelligence in your body than in your best wisdom." - *Friedrich Nietzsche*

Your physical body is the most pristine piece of real estate you'll ever own. For realz. The amount of intelligence that lives inside your body, inside each and every cell is beyond anything we can even comprehend. It is your birthright to fully Love your body and give it what it needs by paying attention and by responding to the messages you receive from it; because it does communicate with you. There's innate wisdom in our body and it speaks to us. The question is, are you listening? Is the line of communication between you and your body open and free of obstructions so you can clearly receive the signals?

That's what we are going to cover in this section, and it has the utmost importance in your Life. Your body temple, your physical body, is nothing less than divine intelligence in physical form. It is the house in which everything else resides – your mind, your heart and most importantly, your soul. When you shift your relationship with your body, recognizing that **your body is indeed the house of your soul**, you will no longer see it as merely a piece of meat with a bunch of tubes in it; nor will you see it as separate from that which we classify as spirit. You'll start seeing your body as the brilliant and intricate piece of art that it is, your connective vessel between heaven and Earth – the vessel in which God's Life force can move through you. By caring for your body, you create the best environment for that Life force to work its brilliance, blessing you with radiant health, presence, clarity, and an elevated state of being.

By applying the different tools presented in this section, you'll begin to shift your lifestyle and bring more attention to the well-being of your body. You'll begin to see that treating your body as a physical temple is indeed part of your divine mission here on Earth at this time. Knowing that, you'll care for your body a whole lot more while noticing the monumental impact it has on the quality of your Life and your connection to everything around you. This is more than just your ordinary healthy diet and exercise regimen – although necessary and part of the deal, we're going after a complete shift in perception and lifestyle, resulting in a complete Life upgrade.

As you begin to develop a more intimate relationship with your body, your attention to your state of balance will increase, since your state of well-being relies greatly on your ability to stay balanced. When out of balance, the intelligence of your body will do whatever it takes to return back to a balanced state, a state of homeostasis. Homeostasis is the tendency of your body to maintain a stable and relatively constant internal environment. Your body, with its innate wisdom, will inform you when something is out of balance, whether it's a physical, mental, emotional and even spiritual.

The more out of balance you are, the louder the message will be. All you need to do is listen and respond as soon as you can.

In essence, balance is a constant state of recalibration. It is not something stagnant or unchangeable. The very same thing which helps you maintain balance and well-being at a certain point in your Life, can very well turn into a disturbing factor in your internal environment.

You can apply this to everything in your Life – any patterns, habits, or lifestyles – all the ways in which you take things in and all the ways in which you use your energy. It can be the food you consume, your physical activities, your exercise routine (or lack of), your sleep patterns, your mental activities, your emotional patterns, your social engagements, your work, your spiritual practice, etc. As you continue to evolve and change, what is needed to maintain a state of homeostasis will change accordingly. You will be able to recognize those changes by observing your state of well-being and any signs of discomfort; those are all indicators your body uses to get your attention. When we Love our body and care for it, we can actually be in touch with it and know what it needs, when it needs it, and how we can make the right adjustments.

Use the following oath as a reminder for yourSelf – a reminder of your dedication and commitment to becoming a living temple. You can write this on a piece of paper and put it somewhere you can see every day:

My healthy body oath:

I believe in aligning daily with my body and using food as medicine to support it.

I believe in the power of my body, mind, heart and spirit and know that they need to be cared for, supported, and nurtured.

I promise to pay attention to the signals my body gives me so that I can make small course corrections and avoid larger breakdowns down the road.

I promise to use my body and health as a platform for creating an extraordinary Life in which I'm living my purpose in the world.

AND SO IT IS!

YOUR BREATH

The quality of your breath has the power to affect the quality of your Life. As simple as that. Yet most people don't pay attention to it, nor do they make the effort to improve it. As with so many other things in Life, our breath is something we take for granted, seeing it as nothing more than an automatic mechanism. And while that is true, it is also our most essential Life giving force. We can survive without food for several weeks and without water for up to ten days. But how long would you last without your breath? Most people can't hold their breath for more than a minute. This simple illustration demonstrates just how essential our breath is; and not only for our basic survival.

So, beyond the fact that we need our breath to actually live, how else can your breath affect your Life? How can something so simple, something we do all the time without even thinking about, be one of the most essential tools you can use to enhance your Life? One of my teachers used to say that *having something doesn't mean much if you don't know how to use it*. You can have the newest, most amazing car sitting in your garage but if you don't know how to drive or if you don't bother to learn, what's the point? Well, that pretty much applies to everything I'm talking about here – learning how to use all that we've been given to the best of our ability.

The moment we bring our awareness and attention onto something, we immediately become more present and aware to the impact it has on us and how we can best work with it. Humans like to search for the most grandiose and sophisticated techniques out there while ignoring what is sitting right under our noses; literally. Becoming aware of your breath and all the ways in which it can help you improve your Life is truly a gift to give yourSelf, especially in the world we live in today. The quality of your breath and your awareness of it must become top priority.

In our modern world, it has been now proven that stress is a number one dis-ease causing factor. Most people in western society live under such an immense amount of stress resulting in physical, mental, and emotional discomforts; and I'm not only talking about the stress of juggling Life and all the different responsibilities we face every single day. Just walking down a busy city street can cause stress in your body, stress you might not even be aware of. As a society, we have gotten used to living under stressful conditions that disturb our nervous system and our body's natural rhythms; and it is far from ideal. We are at a point now where most people in society live in a 'fight-or-flight' state without knowing it.

Fight-or-flight state refers to the body's natural response to either stressful, scary or Life threatening situations. It's a specific biochemical reaction that both humans and animals experience during intense stress or fear. The sympathetic nervous system releases hormones that cause changes to occur throughout the body, the main hormones being adrenalin and cortisol. When those are released, heart rate speeds up and digestion slows down while blood flow gets directed to major muscle groups in order to give the body a burst of energy and strength in case there's a real threat we need to either run away from or fight.

This is a natural mechanism we all need in order to survive, but unfortunately, for most people, it is now activated in situations where that response is not needed, like in traffic or during a stressful day at work. Ideally, once the perceived threat is gone, systems are designed to return to normal function via the relaxation response, bringing the body back to a state of homeostasis. In our times of chronic stress though, this often doesn't happen enough, causing damage to the body in the long run.

The fight-or-flight mechanism is also known as the acute stress response. It is important to understand, as it relates to our day to day Life, that the response can be triggered due to both real *and* imaginary threats. What this means is that the response in your body gets activated whenever you feel anxiety, fear or any stressful situation – your body doesn't know if you're actually facing a deadly animal or simply feeling anxious and stressed out. The same mechanism kicks in to create the exact same physiological changes in the body. The fight- or-flight response is a direct result of adrenaline being released into the bloodstream and anything that causes stress to the body (known or unknown to you) will trigger this response – angry boss, deadlines, family argument, illness, car accident, and even your own fear based and anxiety driven thoughts and beliefs about Life.

It's exhausting and uncomfortable to spend so much time in a state of high red alert. Yet, so many people have gotten accustomed to living in this way. The list of possible physical consequences to feeling stressed all the time is extremely long and varies from subtle symptoms to acute conditions and all the way to serious illnesses. Some of these conditions include: high blood pressure, tension or migraine headaches, digestive issues, hair loss, insomnia, hormonal imbalances (both women and men), emotional imbalances, physical and mental fatigue, sexual dysfunctions and more. Even cancer has been associated with stress and western medicine is finally starting to recognize the connection between the two.

Whether you experience some of these symptoms in your Life or not, as long as you live in this modern world and not in a cave up in the himalayas, you are subjected to stressful conditions and environments. Many people in our society are walking around with either extremely depleted or shut down adrenal glands which causes fatigue and overall low energy. Why do you think coffee is the number one drink in America? When your adrenals don't function in the way they were designed to, you'll need an external stimulation to boost up your energy levels (and if it's not coffee, it's sugar or any other substance to help you feel energized). Moreover, as mentioned above, stress and depleted adrenal glands affect more than just your energy levels.

The more sensitive you are, the more you'll be affected. Some choose to rely on external stimulation, different substances or numbing activities without bringing their attention to the actual cause. They might not even know how much stress their body is under because on the surface things may appear peachy... until the walls come crashing down. On the flip side of that, some individuals who are indeed very sensitive – physically, mentally, emotionally and energetically, choose to live a more secluded

Life and be as removed as possible from the rest of the world. But, if you are anything like me, interested in being a fully engaged participant in the game of Life while maintaining high levels of well-being, your tools must be sharp; and your breath is definitely one of your best tools.

So how do we discharge all that stress? Whether it be actual Life circumstances or your own imagination causing you to feel anxious and stressed out? The answer is simple: *We breathe.* We learn how to breathe deeper, how to breathe slower and how to do it as often as possible. I can tell you for a fact that the day we'll start seeing ads and promotions for deep breathing instead of pharmaceutical drugs and junk food, society's health and well-being will dramatically be enhanced within weeks. Weeks, I'm telling you!

Our breath is the antidote to our stress – not a pill, not a drink, not a smoke, not a snack, not TV or anything else humans use as a "checking out" method; all of these options help us relax, which is why we choose them in the first place. However, we can learn how to live in a relaxed state even in a stressful world by retraining our nervous system. Becoming aware of our breath, taking deeper breaths throughout the day, and doing various breathing exercises, provide a simple and accessible way to help us come down from this heightened state of constant alert and truly relax. Some of the relief and relaxation actually come just from taking a moment to pause and notice what's going on in your body.

So let's cover some of the ways in which you can start improving the quality of your breath, helping you to create an internal environment based on relaxation rather than red alert.

Stop. And take a deep breath...

As much as it is beneficial to do breathing exercises or other breath focused practices, it is also important to sprinkle moments of deep breathing throughout your day, especially when you find your-Self in stressful situations or whenever you notice your body is tightening up. Any time your body contracts with a feeling of uneasiness, that's your signal. In those moments, just pause, close your eyes (unless you're driving of course) and take in the deepest, fullest breath you can with an equally long and extended exhale. It can be one breath or more, as many as you need, but even just one big, juicy breath has a calming effect on your nervous system and your entire body.

It doesn't have to be only when you feel stress or uneasiness creeping in. Get into the habit of sprinkling those deep, intentional breaths throughout your day; it literally doesn't take more than a minute. I know people who actually set up notifications on their phone to remind them to take a deep breath. (Hey, if we're going to use technology might as well utilize it to our advantage).

That one moment of pause, bringing your awareness to the in-flow and outflow of your breath, can shift your entire state of being in an instant. The more you do it, the more moments of relaxation and ease your body gets to in-joy, which will result in a much more relaxed nervous system. When your nervous system is relaxed, you are able to move through Life with more ease, navigating the most stressful situations with a calm attitude, a clear mind and sharp awareness. The opposite of that is a triggered state who's ready to explode at any moment... Over time, those brief moments of pause will turn into a natural state of being – a state in which you'll become more aware of your breath on a regular basis, with the ability to breathe deeper and slower.

Good times to pause and take a deep breath:

- While sitting in traffic (take plenty of deep breaths then)
- While waiting in line somewhere (especially when it's a long line)
- While sitting at your desk at work
- While working on your computer
- While washing dishes
- While preparing food
- While packing to go on a trip
- While cleaning the house
- While outside taking a walk
- While talking on the phone or having a conversation with someone face to face (it's actually quite nice to do with the other person if they're into it)
- Before you're about to have a difficult conversation
- During a difficult conversation
- After you had a difficult conversation
- When feeling upset about something or someone, before you react, take a deep breath.

"Breathing involves a continual oscillation between exhaling and inhaling, offering ourselves to the world at one moment and drawing the world into ourselves at the next..." - *David Abram*

Belly Breathing

This is the most basic of the breathing methods we have at our disposal, and therefore is the one you should master before trying out other techniques. It's very simple, and requires just a few steps:

1. Sit down comfortably, or lay down, depending on your personal preference.
2. Place one hand on your stomach, just below your ribcage. Place the other hand over your chest, on your heart.
3. Breathe in deeply through your nostrils, letting one hand be pushed out by your stomach. You should find that your chest stays stationary.
4. Breathe out through your lips, pursing them as if you were about to whistle. Gently guide the hand on your stomach inwards, helping to press out the breath. (For women, be more gentle with pressing the air out when menstruating or pregnant).
5. Slowly repeat between 3 and 10 times.

You should begin to feel relaxed as soon as you have repeated the Belly Breathing exercise two or three times, but keep going for as long as you wish.

Morning Breathing

While the above exercise can be completed whenever necessary, the next method is to be practiced once you have woken up. It aims to relax your muscles after a good night's sleep, and will help you to minimize tension for the remainder of the day – so you can start as you intend and would like to go on.

1. Stand up straight and, slightly bending your knees, bend your torso forward from the waist. Your arms should be hanging close to the floor, limply.
2. Take a breath in slowly, returning to your original standing position. Move slowly, as you're moving through peanut butter... Head is the last thing to straighten up.
3. Exhale, returning to the position of being bent forward by the end of your exhale. Stand up straight once you have finished, stretching your muscles as required. This can be done as one repetition or can be repeated for 3-5 rounds.

WATER
Hydrated body is a happy body

Since our bodies are made up of about 75% water, they heavily depend on this precious resource in order to function properly – from regulating body temperature to removing waste to lubricating joints to carrying oxygen to the cells. In the same way that low quality breathing affects the state of your well-being, lack of proper hydration has its own consequences. We've all heard the importance of drinking enough water, yet keeping your body hydrated can be done by consuming not only water, but the kind of food that hydrates your body rather than dehydrates it. You actually don't need to drink as much water if you maintain sufficient levels of hydration on a consistent basis. If you find yourSelf feeling thirsty quite often, that's a sign you are not hydrated enough. Fatigue, frequent headaches, high and low blood pressure, constipation, digestive issues, brain fog, undesirable weight gain and premature aging are only a few examples of symptoms caused by a state of low-grade chronic dehydration.

Very often, we can confuse the body's request for hydration with false hunger. The way to shift that is by paying more attention to what feels like real hunger and what is merely a desire to eat; those two are distinctly different. Try drinking a full glass of water whenever the desire to eat arises, at times you know you're not really needing food. Notice if you still feel "hungry" afterwards.

Just like with stress, many people are extremely dehydrated without knowing it. Even if your diet is relatively healthy, you'll be surprised just how dehydrated your body actually is. Over consumption of ANY salty foods, sugary foods, sugary beverages, coffee and cooked food, even of the best quality, contribute to a state of dehydration, making your body overly acidic as well. When the body is too acidic, our well-being suffers; an acidic environment is the perfect environment for health issues to arise as it compromises our immune system, making it easy for toxins and inflammation to take over.

If you suffer from allergies, you might just be dehydrated...
If you suffer frequent urinary tract infections, you might just be dehydrated...
If your blood circulation is not optimal, you might just be dehydrated...
If your joints hurt, you might just be dehydrated...
If your skin is dry or lacking its natural glow, you might just be dehydrated...
If you're constipated more often than not, you might just be dehydrated...

Remember that minor symptoms are the body's way of communicating with you. Instead of waiting for a major health issue or breakdown to occur, become aware of what's going on in your body and start mastering your state of true health and well-being.

So how can we help our bodies stay hydrated and happy?

1. Avoid or decrease the consumption of foods and beverages that dehydrate your body, causing you to play 'catch up' on a regular basis. The main beverages are coffee (especially when consumed in large amounts on a daily basis), and sugary beverages (even healthy beverages with no artificial sugar). Main foods would be packaged food and cooked food when consumed predominantly; cooked food isn't bad, it's just not as hydrating as uncooked and unaltered food which contains a much higher water content. Consuming large amounts of salt (even high quality sea salt), also has a dehydrating effect in your body. Just notice how thirsty you feel after eating a very salty meal. If you find yourSelf feeling thirsty after a meal, that's a sign that the food you're eating is dehydrating.

2. EAT your water: Fluid-filled foods are your winning ticket, the main ones being fruits and vegetables. The less processed your food is (and that includes cooking) and the more alive and fresh it is, the higher is its water content, providing your body high quality hydration. Especially if you're not a big fan of drinking plain water, start increasing your consumption of fresh fruits and vegetables.

3. Smoothies and juices – make it fun and tasty: Blending or juicing your greens, veggies and fruits is a wonderful way to not only get plenty of nutrients into your body, but is also very hydrating.

4. Herbal teas: One of my favorite ways to stay hydrated while also receiving the benefits of different medicinal herbs. You can make a large batch of your favorite herbal tea and sip on it throughout your day.

5. Make your water interesting: Add fresh lemon or lime to your water or

try adding different essential oils, making it more desirable to drink. Essential oils you can experiment with include: lemon, lime, grapefruit, peppermint or different blends that are available on the market.*

Herbs and essential oils are powerful medicine so please find the ones that are beneficial for you, your constitution and condition.

6. Last but not least, and the most obvious of all is to just drink water. However, I encourage you to not only consume water but to consume **high quality water**; that means clean water from a quality source. Spring water is the best source of water you can get, but if that's not available to you, do your best to find the best water source possible and avoid drinking tap water (especially city water), which is loaded with fluoride, chlorine, and other chemicals. Get into the habit of carrying a water bottle wherever you go, making sure you always have water with you (or tea) to keep you hydrated.

FOOD

Make it Alive, Pure & Simple

I want to be clear that the purpose of this section is not to promote any specific diet. Everyone's body is different and there's a time and a place for experimenting with different foods, finding out what your body needs at different phases throughout your Life. However, I cannot deny the fact that the more alive and simple the food we humans consume, the more health, vibrancy, and overall well-being we experience. My Life is a living proof of that and the lives of many I've worked with and continue to work with. Living foods transfer their Life force energy into you which raises you up – in your body, in your mind, and in your heart. Living foods bring you back to Life, reconnect you to nature, and transform your conscious-ness. It's that powerful.

Clean and simple foods like fruits and vegetables keep our cells clean and the blood pure. Fruits and vegetables not only aid the body in cleansing and healing, they also keep the body in top shape; the reason for that is the high water, mineral, vitamin and fiber content. Fruits and vegetables contain high amounts of the nutrients the body needs in an easily absorb-able form in order to function and run smoothly. Most foods people in our society are consuming these days are heavily processed, lifeless, and in-flammatory. Nature's food in its fresh and unaltered state, heals, alkalizes, and strengthens the body. Getting into the habit of eating in this way will completely change your Life and enhance your well-being beyond your wildest imagination.

What you put in your body quite literally becomes you; so what would you like to become? When inspired and motivated to live as a human temple, you'll most certainly start paying more attention to what you consume. If you want to feel aliveness moving through your body temple, if you want to feel clarity and lightness, if you want to fully utilize the potential of your physical vehicle, you must give it the right fuel for that.

Simplifying & lightening up

We need to have a healthy diet to maintain a high level of well-being, yes, but we also need to pay attention to HOW we consume the food we choose to eat and not only the specific food choices we make. This plays a crucial role in the overall simplicity of your Life. Too much food or overly heavy and complex meals, make it very difficult for your body to break down and assimilate the nutrients from the food you're consuming. Even though you're better off with certain food choices than others (because they're much more nutrient dense and satiating), **the level of your physical health is actually dependent on how well your body can assimilate your food intake.**

You know the difference between true hunger and times when you're just eating because it tastes good? What happens then? When we mix too much or go overboard, the food we eat doesn't get digested properly, leaving us feeling uncomfortable. And beside it being uncomfortable, undigested food cannot deliver the nourishment your body needs. It is the *proper breakdown and assimilation* of food that is in fact responsible for delivering all the right nutrients to all the right places. Now ultimately, what's the purpose of eating? To stuff our faces and stimulate our taste buds? I know, some people may say yes to that idea (which breeds gluttony and sickness) but no, we eat to nourish ourselves by ingesting and assimilating all the right nutrients our body needs for its optimum function. So, when food isn't being assimilated correctly, it doesn't matter what you eat, the right nourishment your body needs will be compromised.

Moreover, how you eat profoundly affects the way you feel. Which means a heavy and complex way of eating not only affects you physically, it also affects your mental and emotional state. When looking through our 'wholistic glasses', we can easily recognise how important is the food we consume and the conscious choice to simplify our eating. If you eat light, clean, and simple foods, you will feel light, clean, and simple in your body, mind, and spirit. Too many mixtures encourages over eating which leads to confusion, lethargy, and complacency. I encourage you to not only choose the best and most nutrient dense foods, but to also keep it as simple as possible.

Mixing too many ingredients all at once, eating more than your body needs, and favoring heavy and complex meals more often than not, will result in feeling heavy and over stimulated – body and mind. Yet, so many people don't make that connection. It becomes a cycle that is very hard to break where we turn to food as a means to feel better, usually choosing heavier and denser food to "comfort" ourselves. By doing that, we unknowingly anchor into our cells the very same feelings and thoughts we are trying to escape from or sooth within ourselves.

That's how we can get trapped in food dependencies or addictions, which turn into mental and emotional addictions. After a while we can't even tell what came first – is the craving to eat certain foods is driven by your emotional/mental state or is it the other way around? Start with a simple action step which is paying closer attention to the complexity level of your food consumption and observe the effects your food choices have on you – physically, mentally, and emotionally. Treat your body as a temple and keep moving in the direction of simplicity and health in all areas of your Life.

Start reading labels!

As much as I encourage you to replace packaged food with more fresh, alive, and home-made-with-Love food, I also know that buying packaged or pre-made food can be convenient and extremely helpful at times. Fortunately, we do live at a time where we can find healthy options for packaged or prepared food, making it a lot easier for people to consume healthy meals; this truly makes me very happy. So, if and when you do buy packaged or prepared food, take a moment to read the ingredient list. Make it a habit to find out what it is you're buying and choosing to put in your body.

Not everything that states 'healthy', 'vegan', 'organic', 'non-GMO', etc. is in fact healthy. Not at all. You'd be very surprised to see what's in our food, even what is considered to be a "healthy product". If it has more than 5-6 ingredients, know that it's too much for your body to handle in one shot.

Becoming present, intimate, and intentional with your food

Bringing more focus and attention to the act of food consumption is extremely important. How many times does eating become a secondary thing you do while being occupied with other things? If you usually eat while reading/typing/browsing the web/talking on the phone, etc, I encourage you to become more present and intentional with your food; after all, it is sustenance you're putting into your body so why not stop and be present with it? When you go the a gas station to get fuel for your car, do you put gas in the tank while driving or do you stop your car and turn it off? We all know the answer to that. The food you eat is fuel for your body, so let your body pause for a few moments while filling up the tank. It is indeed an act of Self-Love – your body deserves the time and attention from you while ingesting nourishment.

Avoid consuming food while feeling upset, angry, confused, sad or any other heavy emotion. By putting food in your body while experiencing these states, you are actually anchoring down these emotions into your body and locking them in your cells. Be sure that if you are moving through any emotional stress to first bring yourSelf into a more calm and relaxed state before ingesting food. I cannot emphasize that enough. If need to, take a few moments to breathe and calm down before eating. While eating, put any toxic or heavy thoughts and emotions aside and just focus on your food. Music can be really helpful. If you do find yourSelf stressed, upset or preoccupied in any way, play some of your favorite relaxing music that helps you calm down. Once you feel less triggered, then start eating.

You can become more present with your food by being more intimate with it; after all, it's going into your body, into each and every one of your cells. You can do that by bringing your five senses into the experience of eating. I like to look at my food before I eat it and appreciate it with my eyes. I like to smell my food, even if it's a piece of fruit, and appreciate it with my nose. I am also a huge fan of eating with my hands as much as possible; nothing connects you with your food more than that. Utensils have their place, but they also separate us from the food we eat... and why would you want to separate yourSelf from something that is about to become a part of you? So get your hands in there and in-joy the texture of your food!

Taking it a step further. Before you start eating, infuse your food (and even beverages) with your prayers and good intentions. It doesn't need to be super fancy or complicated. Even just a few words of gratitude for the food you're about to eat and for your body will make a big difference energetically and physically. Your body will break down food much better and you'll feel more elevated and uplifted by the food you consume.

Here's a little prayer I like to use but of course, make it your own and say whatever you feel is right for you:

'Thank you Earth for providing me with this food and thank you for those who grew this food with Love and care.
Thank you food for nourishing my body, mind, heart, and soul.
Thank you body for digesting, breaking down, and assimilating this food in the best way so I can be nourished and satiated.
May every bite nourish every cell of my being and bless me with

radiant health, light from the sun and Love from the Earth.
May all beings around the world be nourished with healthy food
and be blessed with abundance just as I am in this moment.

Thank you, Thank you, Thank you'

MASTERING YOUR SELF-CARE

**Rejuvenation is a way to replenish your energies,
becoming more youthful and happier with yourSelf.**

Your Self-care and learning how to master it goes beyond the basics we
have covered so far. Replenishing your energies **regularly** means that you
give your body the TLC it needs on a consistent basis; it's the necessary
maintenance work your physical vehicle requires. And since the shape and
state of your body affects everything else, a rejuvenated body will result in
a rejuvenated mind, a rejuvenated heart, and an uplifted spirit.

Self-generated Love and appreciation is the fuel that drives us to care for
our bodies. When you learn to appreciate your body as a living temple,
you'll want to care for it in ways you may have never experienced before. From that place, Self-care will become a form of worship rather than
something you feel obligated to do just so you can function. Every act of
Self-care will become a devotional prayer in action. **Every act of Self-care
will be a declaration of gratitude and appreciation for the gift of Life
in a physical body.**

Your appreciation for your physical body will also give you the motivation to look good; which doesn't make you vain or superficial whatsoever.
When the desire to look good is rooted in loving gratitude for your human

body, admiring the image in the mirror is not only acceptable, it is very much encouraged. From my own personal experience, there's a big difference between obsessing over the external shape of your body (based on social conditioning) and the sheer enjoyment of beautifying your physical temple; on the exterior just as much as on the interior.

In-joy caring for yourSelf and your body temple by discovering all the ways in which you can express your appreciation for this piece of art. As always, make it fun, but make it happen. There are many ways in which you can care for your body; what I'm covering here are some of my favorite ways to care for mySelf. These are things I do on a regular basis, have it be daily, weekly, or monthly but I always make it a priority (top priority actually) to incorporate Self-care into my schedule no matter how full or busy it is.

Sleep and Rest

Our bodies all require sleep in order to restore and rejuvenate, to grow muscle, repair tissue and synthesize hormones, and that's only on a physical level. There are more explanations as to why we need sleep, but I'm going to focus on the physical aspect – the importance of giving your body ample **quality** sleep and rest it requires in order to function in the best possible way.

I'm not going to tell you how many hours of sleep to get because that's not the point here; different periods in your Life will require different sleep patterns. Listening to your body and honoring whatever phase you are in is an act of caring for yourSelf. For example, when you're sick, injured, or recovering from something (have it be physical or emotional), you'll need more sleep and rest than usual so your body can focus more on repairing itself. The process of recovery takes extra work for your body which is why you feel more tired. Listen to that. Work with your body and not against it. Slow down and rest more. Doing so will help your body rejuvenate and get stronger a lot quicker.

Since we always want to focus more on quality rather than quantity, aside from giving your body sufficient amount of sleep, you want it to be **quality sleep**. Six hours of quality sleep are by far more rejuvenating and efficient than 10 hours of non-quality sleep. Non-quality sleep is sleep that is not restful – you might be sleeping, but your body is not really resting. If you find yourSelf feeling tired when you wake up even after a long night sleep, take note of that. Your body might not be getting the necessary rest requirements it needs. Also, if you are sleep-deprived because you've been accumulating sleepless or non-restful nights, you can't just log in many hours of sleep to make up for it; although it might help your energy levels in the moment, it still affects your body quite negatively in the long run. The best sleep habits are consistent and healthy routines that allow us, regardless of age or Life circumstances, to meet our rest needs every night.

One of the most predominant reasons for having restless sleep is an over-stimulated nervous system. And although there are many factors which can contribute to that state, I'm going to bring your attention to the top factors I believe to be the most common. You can help your body unwind from the day, calm your nervous system down, and get sufficient and revitalizing rest just by implementing some of these simple habits:

1. *Follow your body's natural rhythms* – Our human bodies, like Mother Nature, function according to natural cycles. These cycles are commonly called the internal body clock or biological clock. When we are out of tune with our biological clock, we're going against the

natural harmony established by Mother Nature. Prior to the widespread use of electricity, people would go to bed shortly after sunset, as most animals do and which Nature intended for humans as well. Therefore, it is **best to go to sleep by 10pm**. I know this is not always possible, but just have that as your 'bedtime' general guideline and follow this guideline as much as you can.

By going to bed early (which means falling asleep before 10pm) you receive the most quality sleep which ensures proper physical regeneration, efficient stress reduction, and restful sleep. One is likely to feel more refreshed with 5 hours of sleep between 10pm and 3am than with more hours of sleep that begin after 10pm. Between **9pm - 11pm,** your body eliminates toxic chemicals from the immune system and between **11pm - 1am,** your liver eliminates poisons and rejuvenates itself. *That is why it is best to be sound asleep by 9pm or 10pm for your body to properly execute these important functions.* Accumulating several restless nights or being sleep deprived for any prolonged periods of time, compromises the natural functions of your vital organs resulting in a weakened immune system, exhausted adrenal glands and heightened stress levels.

2. *Let your body rest, not digest* – To get the proper rest at night, you want your digestive system to be resting and not processing food. If your body is working on breaking down food at night, the quality of your night sleep and regeneration process will be extremely compromised.

   If we follow natural rhythms, the ideal time to have your last meal is **before** the sun sets. It might sounds crazy for some of you who get the munchies at night but this is truly crucial when it comes to your body's ability to fully rest while you sleep. Once it gets dark, the body starts "closing shop" in preparation to shut down and go into resting mode. That's the natural rhythm of our bodies – the more you are in sync with it, the more well-being you'll experience in your Life.

In some places during summertime the sun doesn't set until 9pm. In that case, or when you do eat your last meal after it's already dark, give yourSelf **at least 2-3 hours** between your last meal and your bedtime to make sure you have a few hours to digest your food before going to sleep. Furthermore, it's better if your last meal is on the lighter side, especially if you're having it later in the evening (after 7pm). This guideline alone will make a huge difference in the quality of your sleep and your body's ability to regenerate itself, helping you operate with the highest vitality and clarity.

3. ***Unplug and Relax*** – In our modern world, it's not always easy to follow our body's natural rhythms, especially in a world where we are so far removed from Nature and so plugged into our electronic devices and technology. Electricity and artificial lights make it possible for us to keep on going well into the night after it gets dark, which is wonderful, and at the same time has some implications. As much as technology has its fare share of benefits, it's also a huge culprit in our society's disconnection from Life's natural rhythms (our bodies included). T.S. Wiley and Formby, researchers at the Sansum Medical Research Institute, conclude that: *The disastrous slide in the health of the American people corresponds to the increase in light-generating night activities...*

And I agree with that 100 percent. Moreover, this level of disconnection is ubiquitous, not only in America. Most humans who live in modern society use technology and rely on it so much, they completely ignore their body's internal mechanism. This greatly compromises not only the quality of our sleep but our well-being in general. You don't have to live in a cave or in the middle of the jungle in order to be in sync with Life's natural rhythms and cycles. Living in a natural setting is undoubtedly very helpful, but you can still be connected to your body's natural rhythms even if you live in a city or have a busy lifestyle. You can start by doing the best you can with where you are and soon enough, you'll come to be more in sync with Life's natural rhythms.

At night time, I encourage you to *unplug & relax* – creating an environment for your body to unwind, calm down and prepare for sleep:

- Shut down electronic devices a couple of hours before going to bed or at the very least, an hour before. Checking your emails, browsing the web, or watching tv right before you go to bed is definitely not conducive to your restful night sleep. This is by far the number one thing you want to start paying attention to.

- Dim bright lights and use softer lights or candles once it gets dark.

- Calm your nervous system and body down by drinking herbal tea like camomile or peppermint, play relaxing music, and/or rub lavender oil on your neck, temples and soles of your feet. All of the above is very soothing and calming for your entire body.

- Meditate and be quiet, even if it's 10 or 15 minutes before bed.

These are some basic things you can start with. You can find other ways in which you can relax at night before you go to sleep. Notice how it affects the quality of your sleep and your Life in general – a well rested body is a much healthier, happier and efficient body full of vitality.

Start your day just right

How you start your day is equally important to how you choose to close it:

- If you do need an alarm to wake up at a certain time, choose an alarm that has a pleasant sound rather than a sound that jolts your body and nervous system. Do you really want to encounter stress first thing in the morning?

- After I wake up, before getting out of bed, I like to lay in bed for another 5-10 minutes (or more sometimes) and just be with mySelf in a neutral space of stillness and silence. I usually place one hand on my heart and one on my belly and take a moment to breathe deep and thank my body... feel my body... in-joy being in my body as I lay there. Some days I like to set an intention or simply say outloud that today is going to be a fantastic day, no matter what!

  Whatever you choose to do and however you choose to be with your-Self, just give yourSelf those precious moments between waking up and the new day ahead of you. Avoid checking your phone right away for messages or emails. Give your inner world the nurturing it desires before directing your energy onto anything external. In other words, **take care of yourSelf before taking care of business**.

- Incorporate into your morning routine the kind of practices or rituals that help your body feel energized, your mind feel clear, your heart feel open, and your spirit feel uplifted. It can be meditation, yoga, any kind of movement, or anything that kick start your day in the best possible way.

Move your body daily

A stagnant body is not a happy body so move your body in some way, *every single day*. This is even more crucial if you have a job that requires you to sit at a desk for most of the day or work on a computer for long periods of time. Find the ways in which your body likes to move and pay attention as to what is the most desirable and suitable form of movement you need in any given day.

In general, it's good to do some type of vigorous movement, (the kind of movement that gets your heart rate up and maybe even gets you sweaty), 2-4 times a week. There are so many ways in which you can move your body in this manner – make it fun for yourSelf as well as challenging. Experiment with different activities and switch it up every once in awhile.

Walking is by far one of the best ways to move your body. Long walks (anywhere from 20 minutes to an hour) will do wonders to your physical well-being and beyond. Walking is extremely beneficial for your digestive system, so if things are feeling a bit stuck, take yourSelf out for a walk.

Dancing is another fantastic way to not only move your body but to deeply connect with it. Whether you take a dance class (and it can be any form of dancing) or you just dance by yourSelf to your favorite music, you will feel uplifted and rejuvenated in your body (and in your spirit). Dancing helps break down and move any stuck or stagnant energy you might be holding in your body which makes dancing not only fun but also very therapeutic. Dance like nobody's looking as often as possible! Or maybe everyone is looking but you don't care. Just let go and be ok with being silly!

Stretching your body as part of your daily movement habit is also very beneficial for your physical well-being. If you want to feel good in your body, your body needs to be open, flexible and fluid. Stiffness in the body is extremely uncomfortable and can affect your range of motion quite dramatically. Whether your Life involves a lot of physical activity or whether you have a more sedentary lifestyle, start incorporating more stretching into your day to day activities. It can either be yoga classes, other form of stretching, or even doing some stretches on your own, gently stretching your legs, arms and back on a daily basis.

Get sunlight on your skin and in your eyes

Getting sunlight in your eyes and on your skin has tremendous health benefits but unfortunately, the sun has gotten a really bad rap. In actuality, there is mounting evidence showing that **moderate sun exposure at healthy levels is not only safe, but necessary.** There is absolutely no better way to get enough vitamin D but through sun exposure, both through your skin and your eyes. Many people wear sunglasses most of the time and block their skin from receiving sunlight by using sunblock just because we've been told that the sun causes damage to our health. With all honesty, that is one of the most ridiculous things we can believe in. The sun gives Life to our planet… without it, everything would be dead. So how come the same source that gives us Life is something we need to block and be afraid of? It's absolutely ludicrous.

While wearing sunglasses to protect your eyes from the sun is necessary at times, it is also important to not wear them all the time if you would like your eyes and your body to receive all the benefits that come from our sun's natural light. As long as it's not excessively hot outside, there are actually wavelengths that the sun gives off which benefit your eyes. If you have sunglasses on constantly, your eyes will miss some of the 1,500-some wavelengths that contribute to your eye health. Your eyes know how to take in and utilize full light spectrum which directly affects your brain's hypothalamus, the part in our brain that controls many vital functions. Blocking sunlight by wearing sunglasses too often impacts not only your eyes but your entire body.

If you're someone who does wear sunglasses most of the time, your eyes have probably lost their natural ability to handle sunlight. That doesn't mean you cannot retrain your eyes back to their full capacity. It will take a bit of time to get used to the bright light of the sun, so just start by using your sunglasses less even if it's only a few brief moments throughout the day when the sun is not very strong – early morning or late afternoon is a good time. One of the most beneficial and powerful ways to welcome sunlight into your eyes is by staring at the sun either during sunrise or sunset, when the sun is low. Start little by little. At first you might be able to handle a few seconds but once your eyes get stronger, you'll be able to stare at the sun longer.

When it comes to getting sun on your skin, I encourage you (whenever is possible) to take off your clothes and lay in the sun. 10 minutes a day is all you need, but that doesn't mean you can't do it for longer. Again, early morning or late afternoon is better when the sun is not in its full strength. If you can get ALL of your body exposed, do it; private parts and all. Letting your naked body be immersed in the healing light of the sun is a form of nourishment just as much as food is; and definitely a form of Self-care. Also, unless you're going to be in the sun for an extended period of time, skip the sunscreen. Just like with sunglasses, you want the light of the sun to enter through your skin without blocking it. And if you do need to wear sunscreen, use a natural option rather than any of the toxic chemical based products we see on the market (more on that in a bit).

Everyone is different, of course, but as a general guideline, start befriending the sun by allowing yourSelf to be more exposed to natural sunlight without any filters, screens or blocks.

Your skin – the largest organ in your body

Did you know your skin is the largest organ in the body? As such, your skin deserves attention; lots of it. And not only from a beauty perspective, but from a perspective of health and well-being. Your skin, when being taken care of on a regular basis, will maintain its natural glow and efficacy regardless of age. While our food choices, hydration and quality of breath all affect the quality of our skin, there are additional ways to care for it. Just like any other organ in your body, taking care of it will ensure its proper function.

1. **Exfoliate** – Exfoliating your skin removes dead cells and helps the skin breathe. I use dry brushing on a daily basis and scrub my entire body twice to three times a week using either homemade or all natural body scrubs. Giving yourSelf this treatment is not only very pampering (which is not less important) but helps you maintain the health of your skin and your body.

2. **Use natural products** – To achieve a healthy Life and look good, many people choose to use personal care products. That can be a wonderful thing, but unfortunately, most of the care and beauty products on the market have a VERY high chemical content; even if it says "organic".

These chemicals are very powerful and toxic, and when used regularly, affect not only your skin but your entire body. Putting chemically based products (like sunscreen and other products) on your skin is no different than ingesting chemicals – it gets into your body. You might not get poisoned right away, but your body gets loaded with toxic matter while your skin gets all clogged up.

My golden standard for any products I put on my skin is this: **If it's not suitable for eating, it's not suitable for my skin.** Food based and natural products are the way to go. You can make your own products at home but if that's not your thing, these days, we are very fortunate to have many fabulous alternatives on the market. You can find natural products at health food stores or online. As with food, read the label – if it's an ingredient you can't pronounce or you wouldn't want to put in your body, it's probably not beneficial for your skin either.

Even though I'm focusing on skin products here, this applies to any products you use – hair, oral hygiene, laundry and other cleaning products.

3. **Sweat regularly** – Get sweaty at least a few times a week, whether it's through physical exercise, hot yoga or saunas. Sweating has SO many health benefits beyond just your skin – from expelling toxins to improving blood circulation. The process of perspiring causes your pores to open up as the sweat makes its way through layers of skin to the surface, allowing your body to get rid of toxins through your skin; which is another reason to keep your skin unclogged, ensuring its proper function in the process of toxin elimination. Your skin will not only be healthy, but glowing as well.

Take baths

Things like stress and environmental pollution can deplete your energy levels. One easy way to build them back up is by simply taking a bath. This can be something you do once a week or more if need to. Taking baths is also very helpful in soothing achy muscles and/or joints. Add some Epsom salt to your bath which will help your body relax even more, especially when feeling tight or sore.

Get body work regularly

I find it essential to treat mySelf for a bodywork session once a week or at least once every two weeks. By body work, I mean what is commonly known as massage. Most people see it as mere luxury or something to consider only when feeling tight or achy. However, receiving bodywork on a regular basis is not recommended only because it feels good (which of course, is part of it) but most importantly, to help your body break down tension and stress. It helps your body release toxins and stress that are stored in your muscle tissues and all the way down to your cellular memory. Moreover, working on the layers of your physical body will bring more Life force, vitality, and ease into your mind, heart and spirit.

There are various modalities to choose from, so find a modality and a therapist that resonate with you and your body's needs. My personal preferences are Thai massage, Rolfing, Swedish massage and deep tissue work. For more subtle bodywork and energy work, try Acupuncture and Reiki. Whatever you choose, getting into the habit of receiving bodywork on a consistent basis is a way to improve your well-being exponentially.

Periodical Cleanses

There are truly no limits to what you can achieve on your Life journey as long as it has the support of a healthy and nurtured body that functions at its optimal level. A periodical cleanse is like taking your vehicle in for a tune-up. When it's completed, you can expect to feel clearer, more alive, and rejuvenated on the inside, and more radiant and vibrant on the outside.

The true benefits of doing a periodical cleanse lay in shifting your mind and body to a more central and clearer place while giving your system a chance to detoxify not only your body but your cluttered thoughts and emotional baggage while enjoying less processed, heavy, and stimulating foods.

There are many different cleanses you can choose from. Some cleanses are less extreme than others so it all depends on what your body needs at any given time. Regardless of what kind of a cleanse you choose to do, the idea is to give your body (and especially your digestive system) a break. There are some cleanses which are specifically designed to target certain organs in your body like a liver cleanse or gallbladder cleanse but any cleanse, **when done properly**, greatly benefits your entire body.

You don't need to do a cleanse every month (especially if you eat simple and clean on a regular basis), but a periodical cleanse every 6 months or so will dramatically improve the quality of your Life and overall well-being. Whether you do a juice cleanse, a water fast or simply take a week of eating only raw living foods, will help improve your physical health, your mental clarity and your ability to be more in tune with your body's natural needs and signals.

Connect with nature more often

I see our connection to Mother Nature as a form of Self-care since our physical body is so tightly connected to this great body of Earth. Communing with Nature on a regular basis replenishes and connects us to Life's natural rhythms and cycles which results in greater ease and higher quality of well-being. Spending time in nature is not to be limited to the occasional camping trip but something to incorporate into our daily lives as much as possible. We don't always have the luxury of spending an extended period of time in Nature but don't let that stop you. Connecting with Nature can be as simple as going outside, taking your shoes off and feeling the Earth with your bare feet. That alone can be a game changer.

Every time I spend time in Nature, whether it's a short walk outside, a swim in the ocean, a hike, sitting under a tree, sleeping under the stars or simply putting my bare feet on the grass, I always feel better in my body, heart, and mind. If I feel down, concerned or unclear about something, connecting with nature works like medicine to alleviate those states and to bring me back to my center and clarity of mind.

Finds the ways in which you can incorporate more Nature time into your Life. Just get outside more. Lots more (weather permitting, of course). Be in nature more often, where the air is fresh and you can get away from the hussle and bussle of Life, even if only for a few brief moments. Turn off the tv, computer, and cell phone and go for a walk outside; it is extremely rejuvenating! Smile and be grateful that Mother Earth is always here, waiting for us to join her at any time. The more you live in harmony with Mother Earth, the more harmony you'll experience in your body and in your Life.

"We must awaken while in this body, for everything exists in it."

Create your Self-care structure

What fills up your battery? Physically, emotionally, mentally, and spiritually? What helps you feel more at ease and at peace? What imparts a sense of relaxation in your body and mind? Find the right outlets for you and *plug yourSelf in as frequently as possible.*

What do I do daily?

- Morning ritual
- Evening ritual
- Personal practice
- Personal quality time
- Appreciating and acknowledging mySelf

What do I do on a weekly basis?

- Once a week
- Twice a week or more

What do I do on a monthly basis?

- Once a month
- Twice a month or more

Put in in your calendar if you need reminders – little notifications to remind you it's time to plug your battery in. It will most likely be executed if you actually put it down on paper (or on your device); at least at first if you're just getting used to having a consistent and well-rounded structure that includes your Self-care and personal practice.

Chapter 8

The temple of your Mind – Your mental well-being

"Each of us has a unique mind: unique thoughts, perceptions, memories, beliefs, and attitudes, and a unique set of regulatory patterns. These patterns shape the flow of energy and information inside us, and we share them with others." - *Dr. Daniel Siegel*

Our culture sometimes uses the words *brain* and *mind* interchangeably, even though they do refer to two different things. The brain is an organ; the mind isn't. Some say that the mind resides in the brain but in my opinion, it's not so black and white. However, there is a relationship between our mind and our brain. The left hemisphere of the brain is associated with our thinking, logical mind (also known as the lower mind) and the right hemisphere of the brain is associated with our intuitive, more expansive mind (also called the higher mind). The human mind, as the mysterious creature that it is, is too abstract and multifunctional to be pinned down as a localized thing. If the brain is a vessel in which the electronic impulses that create thought are contained, our mind is used by us to think and understand; but our mind has other functions as well.

One of the more prevalent phenomena in our society these days is the overuse and overstimulation of our thinking-intellectual-logical mind. So many people are either completely disconnected from their body and feelings because they over think everything or they're completely disconnected from the bigger picture of Life; in many cases, it's both. Fine tuning the temple of your mind requires you to first take an inventory of the ways you use your mind: Which functions do you overutilize and which do you underutilize? How cluttered is your mental space and what needs to be cleaned out and refined? This is equivalent to the process of re-programming your computer. You will need to delete some files, update and upgrade some programs, change the software and in some cases – even change the hardware all together.

Once you view your mind as an operating system that has many different functions, you'll be inspired to become more familiar with *all* its functions and learn how to utilize it in the best possible way; doing so will allow you to produce quality results in your Life. Training your mind to use its thinking function more than necessary makes you susceptible to unending loops of overthinking and overanalyzing, leaving you mentally exhausted and stressed out. Being mentally exhausted, stressed out or both, impacts your mental abilities which can affect your productivity and mental clarity in various ways: It can decrease your ability to focus and concentrate for longer periods of time. It can compromise your ability to be decisive, make clear decisions, and find creative solutions in your Life. It can also affect your capacity to assimilate and store much needed information if your mind is too full with concerns and scattered thoughts.

Giving your thinking/logical mind some time off, will help your mind become more relaxed... And having a more relaxed mind will actually help you increase your focus, concentration, creative thinking and mental clarity, making you more productive and efficient with your time. Easing off the over-thinking will also help you access your higher wisdom much more, creating more balance by connecting both your thinking mind and higher wisdom to work together in harmony.

MAKE ROOM FOR YOUR HIGHER MIND TO LEAD THE WAY

"The mind is like a parachute.
It works best when open." - *Frank Zappa*

Our higher wisdom can also be referred to as our intuition which is associated with our higher mind; the more **expansive** function of the mind and one of the mind's most important functions. It is our higher mind which gives us the ability to see the bigger picture and therefore be more connected to our intuition.

The mental drive to understand and figure everything out logically, overpowers the voice of your intuition. Some are more connected to their intuition than others but nevertheless, we all have access to this essential function. The question is, how often do you use it? How often do you listen to it without doubting it or trying to make sense of it? You can read all the books in the world and do an online research marathon but at the end of the day, sometimes there are things *you just know.* That's your higher wisdom – **knowing what you know without knowing how you know it.** But if you are predominantly driven by a desire to understand everything intellectually, habitually giving more power to your thinking mind, you dismiss the higher wisdom of your intuition.

Let's say you are faced with a decision in your Life, maybe even a tough one. A logic driven mind will always try and figure everything out in a rational manner by considering all the facts, by gathering as much information as possible, and by looking for a "logical" route to take. A logic driven mind will continue to think and think about the matter, never stopping to consider that which is not to be found through intellectual or logical thought process. Those 'non-logical' ideas, thoughts, and solutions come from our higher mind; our higher wisdom. It's that stream of information that comes to us at the moment we need it if we can only get out of our thinking mind and listen. More often than not though, if it doesn't make sense logically, it gets ignored, maybe even goes completely unnoticed.

This is not to discredit our logic; it is indeed necessary. However, we must strive to connect our higher mind with our lower mind, our higher wisdom of intuition with our logic and intellect. The function of our lower mind is to zoom in on a subject so it can be understood more clearly while the function of our higher mind is to help us see the the 'invisible' parts of the entire picture; but the higher mind must have the space to do that. How would you be able to clearly see the full picture if you had your face glued to it? When we zoom in too closely on something, we can't see the picture clearly because we are stuck on one angle or point of view; we can zoom in too much to where our view becomes completely blurry.

Creating more space in the temple of your mind for your higher wisdom to be heard, will expand your ability to see more of what is actually possible in Life; that's one of the powers of your higher mind. If your thinking mind plays a dominant role in your Life, a function you keep on overusing or misusing, start moving in the direction of creating more balance. This balance can be obtained by replacing thinking and analyzing everything with the openness to receive answers to your questions from a less logical or intellectual route. It takes practice. If you always use your right arm for everything, of course your left arm will be weaker; but it doesn't mean it can't get stronger with your loving awareness, practice, and dedication. You can help your mind move in a different way, a way that will keep your mental temple focused, clear, open and expansive, fully utilizing its vast potential.

So let's take a closer look at the temple of your mind – what gets to stay, what must go and what will be a beneficial addition…

Obsessive thinking (aka 'The drilling syndrome')

Our logical/thinking mind is indeed a brilliant tool. But just like any other tool, it needs to be used for the right tasks at the right time. For example, having an amazingly powerful and sharp drill will be very helpful for certain tasks yet extremely counterproductive and even destructive for other things. You're not going to use your drill for everything you need to do around the house just because it's a great tool. I doubt you'll use it to unclog your toilet; that'd be a mess!

Our thinking mind is the function we use for our thought process, analysis process, logic based decisions, stored information, black and white facts and so forth. Our thinking mind likes to make sense out of things and find logical solutions; that's its job and it's very much needed for a big portion of our daily lives. But since Life isn't so logical all the time, being stuck in this one function can be very limiting, quite exhausting, and has the ability to turn a tiny hill into a mountain, usually making things more complicated than they are.

As with our drill example, you want to use your thinking mind for the tasks it was designed to fulfill. If you insist on using it for everything in Life, well, you'll be spinning your wheels until they burn. I'm speaking from experience as someone who can very easily fall into the alluring trap of the mind; because it can feel very alluring; like an obsession or an addiction. I've learned (and still learning) how to use my thinking mind **only** for the tasks which require logic. If it's out of my capacity to "figure out", understand or know logically in the moment, the quicker I let it go, the better I feel and the more space I free up in my mind.

My question to you is **where and when do you fall into obsessive thinking? When do you keep on drilling and spinning your wheels only to get stuck deeper in the mud, accomplishing nothing else other than burning your tires?**

Do you over-think decisions you need to make?
Do you over-think your "issues" or "problems"?
Do you over-think that which occurs in your Life?
Do you over-think how you feel?
Do you over-think the unknown future?

Shifting certain mental patterns has made a significant difference in my Life and made me realize just how much energy I was investing (and wasting) on something quite unproductive. The 'drilling syndrome' is very alluring like I said, so if you've trained your mind to overuse this one function on a regular basis, it will continue to do that. That's where the power of our awareness comes in and our ability to shift any patterns we choose. We can choose to give our thinking mind a new training if it's necessary for our well-being. Your mind is not only brilliant, it is also extremely malleable; but it's your choice how to shape it.

Do you like to make assumptions?

It was the book *The Four Agreements* written by the wise Don Miguel Ruiz that brought my awareness to a mental pattern I used to repeat quite often, a pattern that can rob much of one's mental and emotional energy (because those two are tightly connected). By choosing to shift this pattern, I was able to reshape my way of thinking; and oh boy, does that make a difference or what?? Becoming aware of your 'mental traps' will make your Life a lot less complicated, saving your precious mental energy from being wasted in an unproductive manner.

One of the things Don Miguel talks about in his book is to *not make any assumptions*. This one golden principle will save you tremendous amount of time, mental energy, and emotional energy. Now, what do I mean by assumptions?

Going back to our brilliant thinking mind, with its capacity to think logically, it's also a very good story teller. What's funny about most of the stories it comes up with is that to your thinking mind they sound extremely logical and reasonable, maybe even supported by hard core evidence. Our thinking mind can take something completely fabricated and make you believe in it as solid truth… I mean, if it makes sense, why wouldn't you believe it?

And here lies the trap. **When you don't have all the information regarding a situation or a person (especially if you're already feeling triggered by something or someone), your mind will jump in to fill in the blank.** That's its job. It becomes a dangerous territory when we actually believe those "facts" without taking the time to check the validity of whatever stories our brilliant mind has come up with. That's what I call an assumption.

It gets worse when that fabricated fact (which to us might feel like solid reality), triggers an emotional reaction which takes us on a crazy roller coaster ride of more assumptions, more stories, more emotional triggers and the drilling continues on and on...

How many times have you jumped to a conclusion about a person or a situation as a result of either your own beliefs and past experiences, or because a story you heard from someone else? And how many times have those assumptions (or fabricated conclusions) made you spin your wheels for days, weeks, months, and in some cases, years? And how many times later on, have you realized that none of those assumptions and stories were true? And even if it was true, you finally got the opportunity to hear the whole story from the source, only to discover you had wasted precious time spinning your wheels thinking about something that was untrue or quite insignificant.

When we buy into the 'fill in the blank' portion our mind comes up with, when we make up assumptions and stories about someone and/or a situation, we create the space for unnecessary drama to occupy our lives. All those assumptions are like fertilizer for drama to grow bigger and bigger. **The stories your logical mind comes up with are some of the most invasive weeds in the garden of your mind.** And just like weeds in your garden, you want to nip them in the bud. Don't let them grow and definitely don't feed them more fertilizer by making more assumptions on top of your assumptions.

You nip a story in the bud by going straight to the source as soon as possible. If there's something you don't know for a fact, if there's a 'fill in the blank' space in whichever scenario you encounter, I encourage you to NOT fill in the blank yourSelf. Ask the necessary questions, talk to the person or people, get clarity from the actual source rather than other people's 'fill in the blank' stories. Until you know for yourSelf something is true and has actually taken place, you're making assumptions.

Shifting the tendency to make assumptions of any kind will free up tremendous amount of mental space and will also save you unnecessary emotional bumps. Sometimes, it does require courage and a fair amount of vulnerability to ask uncomfortable questions and admit how you truly feel and what you think. However, the outcomes are so much more productive and beneficial.

Some people waste years of their lives resenting or holding on to something that wasn't even real to begin with just because they made up a whole story based on one assumption. That can easily be avoided by going straight to the source to find out the truth for ourselves. It's unfortunate that many of us have trained our mind to stay in the "comfort" of our own stories and beliefs rather than face reality head on. This pulls people out of their authenticity and integrity, affecting the well-being of the individual while disturbing the harmony of our relationships.

If One individual cell has the power to influence the entire system, why not be that cell?

TREAT YOURSELF TO A MENTAL DETOX

"When we constantly expose ourselves to the old, disempowering myths that have wormed their way into books, movies, and newscasts, we end up reliving them by default."

- Alberto Villoldo, Ph.D.

- **Cut gossip out of your Life** – Whether it's you doing the gossip or other people. If you don't have anything beneficial to say about something or someone, better not say anything at all.

- **Cut any negativity out of your Life** – Any information that leaves you feeling uneasy and low can be considered toxic. Being constantly exposed to the information mainstream media puts out there (especially the "news"), does nothing but harm to your mental (and emotional) state. That type of information creates fear, anxiety, and makes people feel powerless. Whatever you expose yourSelf to shapes your perceptions and outlook on Life, so only plug yourSelf into that which uplifts your spirit.

  Another form of negativity is your toxic thoughts about yourSelf. As with gossiping about other people, if you don't have anything nice to say (about yourSelf), better to stay quiet. Also, notice any limiting beliefs you have about yourSelf; what you believe you can or cannot be, do, or have. Don't become a prisoner of your own constricting beliefs either about yourSelf or Life in general. You can start this process by cutting any naysayers out of your Life who tell you what you can or cannot do. Be the empowered one to determine that for yourSelf.

- **Cut complaining** – There's nothing conducive or productive about it. It's totally fine to dislike something or someone in your Life, but what's the point of complaining about it? If you are sitting in a movie theater watching a movie you don't like, sitting in that theater and complaining about how much the movie suck is not going to change the movie (and of course, quite disturbing to everyone else). You're better off walking out of the theater if you can and if you can't leave, take a nap. Or make out with your date. If there's any way you can shift your circumstances, just do it. Don't complain about it. You can use your mind to either find solutions and creative ideas or something negative to complain about... What sounds better to you? If there's absolutely no way to shift your current situation (which can happen), complaining about it definitely won't help you change it any faster.

- **Reduce your visits to social media land** – Social media is a great platform to use but it has also become a pretty polluted neighbourhood and an energy sucker for many. Be mindful as to how much time you spend in that hood and what is the nature of your visits. Do you get sucked into too many debates on social media? Do you let what you see effect you emotionally? Do you go there just to write a few emails only to find yourSelf an hour later (or more) still browsing and looking around?

Social media and the media in general can really fill up our mental space with a lot of junk; so, pay attention. Try taking periodical breaks from social media, other forms of media, and technology altogether. It can be a short break of a couple of days or maybe a couple of weeks if you can. Especially during times in your Life when you need to gather all of your mental focus and concentration, taking these breaks is extremely helpful; crucial actually. You'll be very surprised to find just how much mental energy it actually sucks out of you once you've taken a long break. If you do use social media for your work or business, take your trips there **only** for the purpose of your business; then get out of there as quickly as you can.

• **Information overload** – We are extremely fortunate to live in an era where all the information we need is right at our fingertips. Anything and everything we might be searching for is out there. At the same time, what we consider to be a blessing can very quickly turn into a curse if and when we are driven by 'more is better'.

When it comes to the temple of your mind, notice if you might be in a state of what I call 'Information overload'. The desire to learn and expand is definitely a wonderful thing however, we must recognize when a healthy hunger for expanding our knowledge turns into an endless search. In the same way our digestive system needs time to digest and assimilate the food we eat, our 'mental digestive system' needs the same thing; it needs time to break down and digest the information we take in. If we just keep taking in more and more information without letting it be assimilated, integrated and implemented in the proper way, it doesn't matter how much we take in, it will be blocked from doing what it needs to do; which is to nourish our mind with real wisdom; wisdom we can UTILIZE and put to work.

The mental nourishment you choose to ingest will benefit from the same standards I suggest you have when it comes to the food you choose to eat: first of all, don't feed yourSelf crap and second, choose **quality** over quantity. However, even with quality food (or information), knowing when to stop because it's time to rest and digest is equally important; otherwise, we're just stuffing ourselves.

First step: Discern for yourSelf what kind of information you choose to ingest. Use your own guidance system to feel what rings TRUE for you rather than what is trendy or popular. If something doesn't ring true, don't bother taking it in; like that piece of cake you know is not good for you. If you know you're better off without it, skip it.

By implementing the first step, you'll shift from quantity seeking to quality seeking which will reduce the amount of information you take in almost instantly. This of course will spill to other areas of your Life as you'll start appreciating quality over quantity in your relationships, social interactions, conversations, and different activities you engage in.

Next Step: Once you know the kind of quality information you prefer to ingest, develop your ability to stop; to know when you're full enough and it's time to assimilate and implement. Instead of hopping over to the next teaching, book, workshop or the next best thing on the Internet, assess for yourSelf if a pause is necessary; a pause to integrate. I see so many people going from one thing to the next, ingesting more and more information without stopping for a moment to take a breather. We want to take that which we learn and put it into action. Yes, knowledge is power but **knowledge without actualization is empty power**;

By all means, stay curious and keep exploring new information; the point is not to diminish your curiosity and urge to expand. The invitation here is to find your sweet spot and recognize if in fact you have a strong tendency to jump from one thing to the next without ever stopping to rest and digest. Do you give yourSelf ample time to **implement and embody** that which you learn about or are you constantly hungry for more? More often than not, being overwhelmed by the sea of information out there causes us to lose touch with our innate inner wisdom, which only results in a constant hunger for more.

Choosing your quality information, accompanied by ample time to integrate and implement, will dramatically simplify and purify your mental space. As a result, you will be much more connected to your own inner wisdom. Your inner wisdom is for you to listen to and learn from. Your inner wisdom cannot be heard and felt when it's cluttered and overstuffed with too many other things. As you'll be developing a closer and more intimate relationship with yourSelf, you'll get much closer and more familiar with your inner wisdom and will learn to trust it above all else. All you need to do is make space in your mind and become an attentive listener.

MINDFUL LIVING
The art of being present

The temple of your mind can thrive, become more open and more efficient when its environment is one of presence and mindfulness. Being mindful and present allows us to be more conscious of Life as it happens – not the past, not the future, not any additional stories; just the here and now. Not always an easy task since our brilliant mind likes to try and be everywhere all at once. Some may have strong hang-ups on the past while others may like to jump into the future with their endless to-do lists or worries. For many of us, it's a mixture of both. Anything and everything, but being *present* with who and what is in front of us.

It might sound counterproductive to those who are goal-oriented or have a very full schedule, but cultivating mindfulness will help you achieve your goals and in-joy Life a whole lot more. In fact, you'll become more productive when you live mindfully, present in the moment. Instead of burning your mental energy focusing on either the past or the future, you utilize your mental faculties and focus only on what's needed *right now*. That's not to say you don't make plans for the future and take care of Life's details; of course you do... but not all the time. By becoming more mindful, you will increase your ability to be more present and therefore more intentional and clear.

Approach your mental energy in the same way you approach the time you have every single day – when spending your time in an unproductive manner doing unnecessary stuff, you are left with no time to take care of what's really needed; after all, we only have a certain amount of hours each day. Burning your mental energy in an unproductive way will result in less mental clarity and reduced capacity to focus on what's really important and beneficial for your Life.

Cultivating more mindfulness takes time and practice, especially in our fast-paced society, where we are taught to multitask, run constant lists in our head, and disperse our energy in many different directions. There are simple habits you can adopt in order to bring more mindfulness into your Life. Life is happening in the present moment so let all parts of yourSelf (mind included), be active participants in every one of those precious moments.

- **Do one thing at a time** – I personally Love multitasking and am quite good at it so I'm not suggesting to never do it. However, multitasking can indeed compromise our ability to give 100 percent to the task in front of us. If you do tend to multitask ALL the time (or most of the time), start giving your attention to one single task more often, as opposed to always trying to knock off five different tasks at once. When you're driving, just drive. When you're eating, just eat. When you're writing an email, just focus on that email. Your mind might go nuts wanting to pull you in many different directions but I promise you, it does get easier with time and practice; you'll discover just how much more productive and efficient you can be without needing to always multitask like a circus performer.

- **Deliberate and mindful action** – As you focus on one task at a time, also take your time with it. You can focus on what's infront of you but if you're rushing it because you're already thinking about the next thing you need to do, you are still multitasking – mentally multitasking. Instead, move slower and pay full attention to the task at hand. Make your actions deliberate and mindful rather than rushed and scattered. Practicing that will dramatically increase your focusing abilities and mental clarity.

- **Everything becomes a meditation** – Meditation is a practice of concentrated focus upon a sound, object, visualization, the breath, movement, or attention itself in order to increase awareness of the present moment. Although carving time to just sit and meditate is a wonderful tool to help you cultivate more mindfulness, everything you do can become a form of meditation – cleaning, cooking, walking, eating, driving, browsing the web, talking on the phone, gardening, making Love… Everything we do, from the most undesirable chores to the most enjoyables activities, is an opportunity to practice mindfulness. Start putting your entire mind into all that you do and do it slowly and completely. Let yourSelf be immersed in it, fully in-joying the present moment.

- **Do less and create space** – How can you possibly do less when you're busy and have a long 'to-do list'? Well, it makes you look at what is or isn't important. When you let go of what is not a priority in your Life (based on your well-being), you are able to do less and **invest your energy in quality rather than quantity.** The need to constantly be busy is a social epidemic and for many of us, acts as a mental addiction. In that case, the busyness of Life becomes a drug; an external stimuli. Letting go of the need to constantly fill your days with to-do lists, appointments, meetings, etc will allow you to lead a full and rich Life while experiencing spaciousness and relaxation. And even though some days may be more full than others, as a guideline, start creating more space in your Life by discerning what is or isn't enriching for you.

- **5 minutes a day of nothing** – It can be a deliberate meditation or simply taking a few moments to just sit in silence. Become aware of your thoughts and focus on your breathing. Observe the world around you; you'll be amazed how much your busy mind can benefit from this simple practice. If you'd like to take this a step further, as much as possible, spend time alone in Nature doing nothing. Become comfortable with the silence and stillness and train your mind to simply in-joy the present moment.

- **Pay attention to who's in front of you** – Many of us are accustomed to be more in our heads than with the person in front of us – if it's thinking about what we need to do in the future or thinking about what we want to say next. Either way, we can't be present with the person in front of us and really listen to them if we're too occupied thinking about the next moment (or next week or last year). Bringing your full presence to every conversation and every person you come in contact with, gives you the ability to fully in-joy that person. In the case you find yourSelf not enjoying the interaction, mindfully end it; which takes your present awareness as well.

- **Tame the wild worry monster** – Very often, thinking about the future involves worrying about it. Regardless of what the subject of worry is, worrying is a harmful virus to your system, a nasty pollutant to the temple of your mind. If there's nothing you can do about something in the moment, what's the point worrying about it? Worries breed anxiety which is extremely toxic to your well-being. So, if you tend to worry about the future more often than not, become aware of the worry monster in your head and recognize when it has gone wild. When you catch it, practice bringing yourSelf back into the present moment by taking a deep breath and say: *Everything ALWAYS works out perfectly. All is well.* It takes practice, practice, practice. Soon enough though, this wild monster will turn into a little gold fish within the temple of your mind.

How you choose to spend your mental energy is a choice just like any other; and making choices always leads back to your relationship with yourSelf – **do you Love and value yourSelf enough to make the best choices as it relates to the temple of your mind?** If you spend most of your mental energy in any of the ways I've described, where does it leave your mental reserves, capacity, and focus? What shape does it leave the temple of your mind in?

Become present and open your mind to see the many roads Life offers. Let go of the worries, excessive thinking, excessive information input, and any other distractions so you can be clear on what really matters to YOU; and what *does* really matter to you? Being present is undoubtedly a way to in-joy your mind and your Life to the fullest. By being mindful, by being present with Life, you'll start enjoying your food more, your friends and family more, and pretty much anything else you do. When truly present, even things like washing dishes or driving can turn into a source of immense fulfillment. In this way, you can start using your mind as a tool to enhance the quality of your Life rather than the opposite; and that's exactly what your mind was designed for.

Chapter 9

The temple of your Heart – Your emotional well-being

"In order to heal we must feel…"

We are living in some of the craziest times in human history. There is a massive awakening taking place, both individually and collectively, as we are ushering in a complete paradigm shift. More and more individuals are waking up to the fact that much of our true divine nature as human beings has been suppressed for many generations by the patriarchal structure of our modern society. This structure has been a dominant force on this planet affecting all of us as individuals, as a global family, and of course, our precious Mother Earth. The patriarchal structure is a system in which males hold the primary power. Although there's nothing inherently wrong with that system, we are now facing the consequences of living way off balance for the last hundreds, if not thousands of years; the pendulum has swung so far off to one side, it has actually gone missing; but we are slowly finding our way back.

Living under the influence of a patriarchal structure has caused us, as a global network, adopt a very masculine approach to Life, regardless of personal gender. A masculine approach is driven by logic, practicality, straight facts, less feeling-more thinking, goal-oriented mindset, external achievements and "success", competition, desire to conquer and reach the top no matter what. What we are starting to recognize is that there's a healthier, more wholesome way to work with this masculine approach. With this new awareness, we are now seeing the value of the feminine approach, an approach that is based on feeling our way through Life rather than thinking our way through it; an approach that not only recognizes human emotions, but acknowledges how valuable they truly are. An approach that focuses on *internal achievements and success* just as much as external. It's a gentler, more relaxed approach to Life and most importantly, it's a heart centered approach full of compassion and Love.

We are all learning, individually and as a society, to live more from our heart. We are learning how to work constructively with our human emotions rather than suppressing them, denying them, or letting them completely run us over. We are learning how to feel more; how to feel our pain with Love and compassion. We are learning that **our true and profound healing resides only within the temple of our heart, healing that leads us to freedom** – freedom from social conditioning, suppression, shame, guilt, fear, anger, unworthiness, and the programs playing in the background telling us to hide who we truly are. We are learning how to give ourselves permission to not only feel but to express the full range of our human emotional scale – from ecstatic joy to extreme sadness, knowing each emotion has something to teach us if we are only open and willing to listen and learn.

Living from the heart doesn't suggest we discard our logical thinking. It's more about creating harmony between our mind and our heart, bringing them to work together rather than existing in a state of constant battle. In my view, this is one of the most important tasks we are here to master. Because on a deeper level, it's about bringing the masculine and the feminine to work together in unity; and that starts with each and every one of us. It doesn't matter if you are a woman or a man, we all carry within us both masculine and feminine energies: thinking vs. feeling, logic vs. intuition, taking action vs. a passive approach, etc. Since we have swung so far off to one side, there must be a concentrated period of time where we must pay closer attention to our feeling-based, more feminine, emotional nature; just so we can come back to a healthy center point. As with everything else, the big shifts on a global scale will be seen and felt when enough of us learn how to master this.

MASTERING YOUR EMOTIONAL WELL-BEING

So, let's take this one step at a time. In order to live more from our heart and improve our emotional well-being, we first must create a dialogue with our emotions, which is only possible by feeling ALL of our emotions and by learning what it is they're telling us. Each emotion has a message for you – sadness has something to show you just as much as joy. Anger has something to show you just as much as neutrality. Depression has something to show you just as much as happiness.

If you don't know what it is you're feeling or if you keep suppressing, denying, or pushing away certain emotions (because they're not comfortable or pleasant), mastering your emotional well-being will be quite difficult. Moreover, doing any of the above will also block you from connecting with your heart and truly heal from within; and we heal from within by healing our emotional wounds, especially the ones buried underneath the surface. That is one of the keys to attaining emotional well-being. And if we want to *maintain* our emotional well-being, we must have an open dialogue with our emotions.

In order to create a healthy dialogue with our emotions, we need to develop emotional intelligence. Emotional intelligence is the ability to feel, identify and manage your own emotions and the emotions of others. It is generally said to include two skills: **emotional awareness** – the ability to harness emotions and apply them to tasks like thinking and problem solving; and the **ability to manage emotions**, which includes regulating your own emotions and emotional needs, lifting up or calming either yourSelf or other people.

It is vital to not only develop your emotional awareness, but to *track the actual root* of your emotions, especially emotional patterns which you find yourSelf repeating again and again. Without this piece, our emotional awareness is incomplete and can cause us to go around in circles. We must remember that much of the emotional triggers we experience presently in Life are actually rooted in the past. For that reason, I like to follow the same thread over and over again: *Treating yourSelf as a little child who's asking for attention, Love, and nurturing.* That's always the foundation, especially when it comes to something as vulnerable and sensitive as your emotions and your heart.

We each encounter different challenges when it comes to our emotional world – some may have a hard time being in touch with their emotions while others may be so overruled by them, it affects their lives in a non-beneficial way. As someone who used to identify more with the latter, developing my emotional intelligence has been one of the most vital skills on my healing journey. This skill has helped me to know mySelf and my emotional world much better and therefore reshape the way I live in the world.

You see, I am a very sensitive and emotional creature and my emotional world is rich and full. In any given day I can feel the entire spectrum – from sadness, fear, and anxiety, to joy, calmness, and complete ecstasy. As a sensitive creature who feels so much and so deeply, it is easy to get affected by Life's circumstances and my emotions can very quickly take the front seat and rule my Life; and that was my reality for many, many years. I would take things very personally which got me stuck in a perpetual cycle of Self-loathing, feelings of unworthiness, and severe lack of Self-esteem; all of which kept the demon in my head very much alive telling me I wasn't good enough. Comparing mySelf to everyone else (only to find faults and imperfections) was my drug of choice. As a result, I would go through many highs and lows, emotional turmoils, and periods of depression. The frustrating thing was that I didn't have full awareness as to *why* I was trapped in that cycle.

Lacking true understanding of the source for my emotional patterns affected my decision making process, my actions, and my perceptions of mySelf and the world around me. I now know that the eating disorders and distorted body image I dealt with for many years stemmed from this underlying issue – lack of awareness to the real cause of my emotional pain. This lack of awareness caused me to easily be swayed by my emotions, and more often than not, in a destructive, Self-sabotaging way.

Developing my emotional intelligence didn't diminish my sensitivity nor did it suppress my emotions; it has simply helped me turn my sensitivity into a blessing as opposed to a curse. Now days, as a result of an increased emotional awareness, I use my emotions to guide me in a constructive way by seeing each emotion as a messenger with a message for me. Instead of letting my emotions rule my Life, I now acknowledge that which I'm feeling, the root cause of any particular emotion, and how can I best attend to my heart (which is usually a time to give mySelf more Love instead of reacting to any given emotion or experience). The ability to understand and treat the cause of my emotional patterns has been my saving grace. It has paved the way for me to attain emotional well-being without alienating mySelf from my emotions and emotional nature.

There are many people who claim to have a well-developed emotional intelligence, yet they completely disregard the child within them. That version of emotional intelligence will not take you very far. Without tracking the root of what it is you're experiencing on the surface, you'll keep missing the actual target. Think about a garden. If you have weeds constantly popping up, the only way to fully eradicate them is to dig deep and find the roots; otherwise, they'll keep coming back. If you only chop the part you see on the surface, it does the trick for a little while, but they'll just pop back up again. Same thing with our emotional patterns that keep us looping around and around in pain and emotional anguish.

With that in mind (and heart), start assessing your emotional garden – what are you growing and cultivating that is beneficial and what are some weeds to pay attention to? Where do you need to dig deeper in order to find the root? It will also be beneficial to recognize where do you stand on the scale to begin with:

• How well are you in touch with your emotions? Do you recognize your emotions as you experience them or is it only in retrospect that you are able to identify how and what you were feeling in the moment?

- How much do you let your emotions run the show? Does your emotional state affect your Life in any destructive way? Does it hinder your ability to make the best choices and decisions for your Life? Are you able to find the connective thread between those emotional patterns and your child-Self?

- Do you feel emotionally balanced? Are you able to feel ALL of your emotions without suppressing them, denying them, numbing yourSelf from feeling them or on the flip side, reacting to them too impulsively?

Once you identify your starting point, you'd be able to see where you are challenged in your emotional world and what it is you need to address the most. It has been shown that our ability to understand and manage our emotions plays an important role in our decision-making process, which can dramatically impact our lives either positively or not. If you keep making decisions based on emotions that you're not in touch with or, conversely, are overpowered by, you'll find yourSelf in recurring situations that don't enhance your Life. What I'm about to take you through are some of the biggest emotional triggers most of us experience in Life which can become a source of emotional pain and toxicity. **The heart cannot fully open up in a toxic environment or if you're unknowingly addicted to emotional pain.**

It takes courage to face our wounds, to feel our pain, and to understand where it's all coming from. Not for the faint of heart, no. But what's on the other side of this courageous journey is so much freedom, so much joy and most importantly, so much *real* Love.

Do you take things too personally?

To truly master our emotional well-being and Life in general, it is essential we live within the **human experience,** without getting lost in the **human condition.** There are some things we are conditioned to think, feel and do, which are necessary for our survival and helpful for our expansion. For example, when you feel a threat is coming, you walk away. When you have an inspiring idea, you follow the inspiration. When you feel drawn to someone or something, you investigate the source of attraction. However, not all that we are conditioned with is equally beneficial or productive. It takes skill to identify which of our human conditionings is helpful and which is merely a trap.

One of the biggest traps within our human condition is taking things personally; it's a trap most of us default back into, knowingly or not. It acts as a malfunction within the human experience which can result in some major emotional turmoils, leading to potentially difficult and painful situations. When we take what others say or don't say, do or don't do personally, we automatically feel 'less than' or down, as if our sense of Self-worth is compromised. This condition is rooted in the belief that everything is about ME... And who would you say sees reality in this way? Little children, right? As I've already mentioned, there's a little child within every adult.

Taking things personally creates an internal discomfort and can get even more complicated when it turns into an angry conflict with another. Depending on where you stand on the emotional scale, there are various ways how taking things personally may look like for you. You may completely shut down because of something a person had said or hadn't said, done or didn't do. You might react impulsively because you feel offended or hurt.

You may feel the need to hurt someone back in some form of revenge (consciously or not). Regardless of how it shows up in your Life, it's essential to know that even when we do feel hurt by someone or something, it's still not a personal thing. Any emotional trigger or pain you experience is merely an **opportunity for you to bring your attention to the *source* of that pain;** and the source is your inner child. The source goes back to any emotional wounds that are still open underneath the surface of your awareness.

What on the surface may feel like an emotional reaction to someone else's choices, words or actions, if we dig deeper, we find that little child again sitting in the dark. It's the same little child who truly believes that everything revolves around them, equating Love and their sense of Self-worth with how much attention (either positive or negative) they receive from their environment. If your relationship with yourSelf isn't strong enough, when you don't give yourSelf the Love and care you desire in your Life, you don't only look for external sources to provide you with that, but you also fall into the trap of believing that other people's opinions, words or actions somehow demonstrate a lack of Love; that somehow the choices of others are about you or are a reflection of your worth.

Choices others make, words others say, and actions others take do affect us, yes, it's very natural. Yet, it has nothing to do with you on a personal level and it certainly doesn't say anything about your value or worthiness. Each individual lives in their own personal world and is operating according to their own beliefs, views, feelings, value system and so forth. Even if someone says or does something which to you may feel painful, hurtful and even heart breaking, you must realize that they're making their choices based on their own world view, not yours. If you are affected by every single thing people think, say or do, if you're living under the impression that your worth is determined by the world around you, you're insisting on putting yourSelf through an emotional war zone within.

In his book, *The Four Agreements*, Don Miguel sums it up so beautifully:

"As you make a habit of not taking anything personally, you won't need to put your trust in what others say or do. You will only need to trust yourSelf to make responsible choices. You are never responsible for the actions of others you are only responsible for you. When you truly understand this and refuse to take things personally, you can hardly be hurt by the careless comments or actions of others.

If you keep this agreement you can travel around the world with your heart completely open and no one can hurt you. You can say I Love you without fear of being ridiculed or rejected. You can ask for what you need. You can say yes or you can say no – whatever you choose – without guilt or Self-judgement. You can choose to follow your heart, always. Then you can be in the middle of hell and still experience inner peace and happiness. You can stay in your state of bliss, and hell will not affect you at all. "

I know this is a tall order but I promise you, it will transform your Life. This doesn't mean you'll stop feeling hurt, pain, or disappointment. We can experience all these emotions without letting them throw us out of our center and into the abyss of Self-doubt, Self-defeat or extreme low Self-esteem. This is all coming from my personal experience, my friend. As someone who lives with her heart wide open, trust me, it is easy to get it shattered. Those experiences though, and the people who played their part, have helped me get more rooted in my own sense of Self-worth and Love for mySelf, recognizing that no matter what the person in front of me chooses to do or not do, is not about me no matter how personal it appears.

Emotional maturity – let go of emotional drama

Your emotional well-being depends on this important guideline. Let that be your north star when navigating through the emotional ocean of your Life. Emotional drama not only makes Life a lot more complicated, it also creates massive amounts of stress in your Life (and what did we say about stress? Not invited to the party). **Anything which is a source of drama in your Life can be considered toxic.** Emotional toxicity will affect you emotionally, of course, but will also affect your physical body sooner or later. Very often, what western medicine defines as a physical condition is actually a result of a suppressed and/or toxic emotional state. For your emotional well-being and overall quality of Life, adopt what I like to call the **'zero drama policy'** approach.

What is emotional drama? Pretty much anything that feels like a soap opera episode; anything that feels like emotional heavy weight you're trying to lift with one arm. Emotional drama can be generated internally or externally. The Self-generated type is internal turmoil you are creating within yourSelf (which more often than not, ends up playing out in some complicated manner). The external type is generated by other people, sucking you into it. Either way, finding yourSelf in the midst of an emotional drama more often than not is an emotional pattern that is worth being recognized.

Similarly to our mental patterns, our emotional patterns can be just as addictive. I know the word addiction sounds extreme, but it's a real thing.

As an individual and as a society, if we want to evolve and make some significant changes, we must acknowledge that emotional addictions are as real as any other substance or drug addictions.

It has been scientifically proven that our brain releases specific chemicals every time we engage in any sort of an activity, whether it's physical or not. When we are engaged in some sort of an emotional episode, our brain gets stimulated in a way that brings us pleasure and satisfaction (consciously or not). It's that feeling of pleasure and satisfaction that keeps us coming back to the same loop; hence, we form an addiction. Unconsciously we get addicted to the emotional turmoil and even the pain that comes with it. Recognizing these loops and more importantly, understanding that the root cause of these emotional addictions is a wounded and neglected inner child, gives us the ability to face these patterns heart on (and head on).

Ask yourSelf if you are indeed addicted to emotional drama (internally, externally or both). Does your Life look like a series of soap opera episodes and do you find yourSelf needing to put out emotional fires quite frequently? Do you find yourSelf attracted to people or environments that like to start those fires? How much of your time and energy do you spend dealing with complicated situations that started as something simple but were blown out of proportion as a result of false assumptions, taking things personally, miscommunication, lack of integrity, lack of honesty, lack of authenticity or playing games?

Emotional drama can be a thing of the past if you choose to live in a state of **emotional maturity**. Emotional maturity is your emotional intelligence in action. It is a choice to rise above the human condition and the temptation to indulge in any kind of toxic situations and emotional patterns that drain you. Do you remember the bouncer who's standing at at the door of your temple? Your Love for yourSelf will keep the drama or any potential drama at bay. If and when emotional turmoil does occur, instead of getting sucked into it, you'll know how to handle it with maturity or when necessary, remove yourSelf from the situation altogether.

You are moving in the direction of true well-being and simplicity, so let that be your guiding light. Remember though, simple doesn't always mean easy; Life isn't easy all the time. You will encounter difficult situations which will bring up difficult emotions for you to deal with; however, it doesn't need to become complicated or turn into an emotional shit storm. The way you choose to deal with difficult situations and emotions will determine that part. Choosing emotional maturity will be your winning ticket every time, even though you might feel tempted to resort back to the thrill of an emotional storm. Keep in mind that storms do bring massive destruction whenever they hit, resulting in a big mess to clean up afterwards. And although destruction and pain are necessary for our growth and the opening of our heart, Life will naturally present that to us; we don't need to seek out any additional messes to clean up.

There are some key points I believe to be essential to our emotional maturity. I offer them to you as guidelines to live by in order to move in the direction of mastering your emotional world and enhancing your emotional well-being:

1. **You're not here to save anybody** – The savior complex will very quickly pull you into overly dramatic (and toxic) situations. You cannot help anyone who doesn't want to be helped and is not willing or ready to take the necessary steps. Sometimes supporting a person's

journey from afar is the highest form of Love you can choose to give, not just to the other person, but first and foremost to *you*.

More often than not, this 'savior complex' is an unconscious motivation and not something we are aware of. So, for those of you who are naturally very loving and caring, examine this area in your Life and be honest with yourSelf: **do you find yourSelf playing or wanting to play the role of a savior in people's lives**? Regardless of the state you're wishing to pull that person out of, if the person is not able or willing to meet you in the middle, you'll keep being pulled down along with that individual no matter how emotionally strong you are. The belief that you are here to save someone will take you down a bottomless pit of emotional turmoil.

If your well-being remains your top priority, there are times when removing yourSelf from a situation or a relationship is the best choice you can make, as challenging as it may feel. In order to do that and not get caught up in the 'let me save you' game, you must have your Self-worth in the right place. You also need to have clear and healthy boundaries. When you don't, things can get complicated and emotionally draining. Your emotional bandwidth is very valuable so use it wisely. Know that **no one needs to be saved, we all just need to be loved.** Love yourSelf enough to make emotionally mature choices rather than rehashing emotional patterns and know that taking a step back from a situation, when necessary, is indeed a form of Love.

2. **Don't play games** – Be real, transparent and authentic with yourSelf and others. Honesty and transparency are not only integrity's best friends, but also the foundation of our emotional maturity. Ask for

what you need, state what you want or don't want, be honest about how you feel and who you are. Don't try to guess other people's needs and feelings and free others from trying to guess that about you. Just be real. It has a lot to do with your ability to be authentic, speak what is true for you, and be able to receive other's truth without taking it personally.

Wearing a mask and hiding the truth only works short term and will ALWAYS come back one way or another to bite you in the ass. Moreover, not being real or honest is quite toxic to your emotional well-being, which, in the long run, becomes an energy drain underneath the surface and a huge block to your heart. The more you try to hide your true feelings, the more murky the waters get, within yourSelf and with others. As uncomfortable or unpleasant it may be, the truth does indeed set us (and others) free.

3. **Clear and heart centered communication – the magic solution –** Emotional maturity definitely requires us to not only be aware of our own emotional state, but to also be able to express it in a way that allows others to see where we're coming from. The ability to express your needs and emotions is extremely vital for your own personal well-being and for the health of your relationships. Therefore, knowing how to identify different needs and emotions at different times is very valuable; if you can't do that with yourSelf, how would you be able to express it to someone else? That someone else can be your friend, your parent, your child, your partner, your boss, or anyone you come in contact with.

When we don't express our true needs or feelings, they turn into resentment (especially when suppressed for an extended period of time). That's how people get to a place where they can easily explode on someone else, even for the tiniest thing. Anger is nothing more than repressed or suppressed passion so any emotion, need or desire we suppress, can very easily turn into anger and frustration when not expressed properly.

In a clear and heart-centered communication, you first identify that which you feel or need to then communicate it to whomever you're dealing with in the moment. For example, if you're feeling sad and as a result you need to be by yourSelf (or whatever needs arise for you), be clear with the other person and just say it as it is: *'I'm feeling sad and I need to be alone for a little while.... or I need a hug.... or I need someone to just be with me without saying anything.'* Don't expect other people to read your mind or your heart. It does take a certain level of vulnerability, not hiding how you truly feel and what you truly need; indeed, a more feminine approach. But this approach can help us attain harmony even in the most difficult situations or when we're moving through difficult emotions.

In heart-centered communication, we emphasize *listening*. As much as we want to be heard and received, it's essential we do the same with others. If the mind wants to come up with answers, solutions, and in many cases, defenses, the heart just listens. You may disagree with the other person, but you let that person express themselves without passing judgment on their experience and without taking it personally. Clear and heart-centered communication focuses on listening, honoring, and receiving ourselves and one another.

Adopting this approach also helps us let go of the relentless need to be right. That alone can really drive us mad sometimes. How much of your emotional juice do you invest in needing to be right? Is it really worth it? If you're finding yourSelf facing a dead-end with someone, the more emotionally mature choice would be to let it go rather than to keep on digging. You'll be the one to discern in every situation what's the best course of action. In general though, I can't even tell you how many times in my Life the choice of letting something go (instead of proving a point), brought the greatest amount of peace into my Life; and of course, helped to restore the harmony within the relationship as well.

I guarantee you, the more we adopt this way of communicating with one another, the less conflicts we will experience in our personal lives and in the world. It starts with each of our personal ability to develop our emotional intelligence, to understand the root of our emotions, emotional patterns and needs, to increase our emotional maturity, and to accept the way we and others feel in any particular moment. With that kind of approach, clear and heart-centred communication will take place naturally. We can and will have disagreements but they will be handled very differently. If no one is trippin' on being right and just expresses their truth clearly while listening wholeheartedly to the other person, how complicated can it get? Everything becomes a lot simpler as a result and a lot more loving. We can have our differences, but that doesn't mean we can't live in harmony; and to do that, we must learn the way of the heart.

THE WAY OF THE HEART

"If you come back to yourSelf, you will find your heart. And to be nurtured and oriented by your own heart is the most glorious thing possible. It's the sweetest, most fulfilling, most joyful, blissful way to be. When you look there, you'll see everything."

- 'The Magician Way' by William Whitecloud

Getting closely familiar with the way your emotional world operates allows for healing of deep emotional wounds. Emotional wounds have the power to affect your sense of Self-worth and your ability to receive and give Love in its purest form. That's the reason why many of us build guards and shields around the heart. As long as that wounded inner child sits in the darkness of your unconscious, you're not going to feel safe enough to take the guard down. But when we lean in and dive into our emotions and most importantly, into our pain instead of running away from it, we create a safe, wise, and mature internal environment for the heart to open up; and an open heart is indeed the essence and wellspring of Love.

Our heart is like a treasure sitting in the bottom of the ocean. We must dive in and face the darkness and the uncertainty of this vast ocean in order to reach the treasure. But how can we dive in if there are shackles and chains keeping us tied to the dock? How can we dive into the depth of our emotional ocean if we're too scared to leave the safety of the surface? If we're too scared of what we may find along the way? If we're too scared of our own sea monsters?

The way of the heart teaches us how to feel our fears and embrace them with compassion. It teaches us to Love and accept our insecurities and get in touch with our deeply ingrained sense of unworthiness. It asks us to face all of our sea monsters – all the ways in which we sabotage our true expansion and receptivity to Life and all the ways in which we block Love. You cannot let true Love penetrate your heart if you don't feel worthy of it. You cannot see that you are indeed a child of God who is loved in every possible way if an old program of inadequacy is still playing in the background. By allowing yourSelf to feel your pain or any uncomfortable emotion, you heal from it. By allowing yourSelf to heal, you reconnect to the treasure of your heart.

Within the treasure of your heart, as unfamiliar as it may feel or maybe even disorienting, you'll find all the Love and the compassion you need for yourSelf and for others. There you'll find true joy and true fulfillment that is not dependent on other people or any external sources. There you'll find the relaxation and the ability to let go of control, let go of codependency, let go of addictions (be it mental, emotional or physical), let go of emotional pain, fears, insecurities or anything else that keeps you feeling separate from the totality of Life. Your heart will become your guide, reminding you that Love is ALWAYS the answer no matter what the question is. Once guided by Love, trust your inner wisdom and clarity of mind to show you how Love needs to be expressed in any given moment. But no matter what, Love must feed into all aspects of your Life in order for you to achieve true fulfillment, starting with loving yourSelf deeply and unconditionally.

"You have to lose yourSelf totally before you can come to your heart. The mind orients itself by sticking to what it knows from the past, whereas the heart gets its knowing from the moment. The heart steps outside the past to include all possibility. That's the only real truth, and you have to learn to Love the disorientation that opens you to it…" -*'The Magician Way' by William Whitecloud*

Our ocean of emotions which we need to enter in order to reach our heart is anything but rational or predictable. That tells you a lot about what you can expect when you choose to embrace the way of the heart; you won't always find logic there. More often than not, there's no rational or logical way to explain that which you are feeling… How in the world can you explain the indescribable? How can you begin to describe the feeling of immense ecstasy within you, so immense it causes you to burst out laughing without any "apparent" reason except for the sheer joy of being alive? What words can truly convey the feeling of being deeply touched by the beauty of Life, such glorious beauty it brings you to your knees in tears of gratitude and awe? Others may think you've gone mad, but you know you've reached places within yourSelf that are truly beyond anything the mind can even comprehend, let alone rationalize.

Words do fall short where the heart is concerned. Let yourSelf feel all of who you are without the need to explain or reason what it is you are feeling. When you feel sad, cry. When you feel joyful, laugh. Give yourSelf permission to laugh uncontrollably and let tears come down your face without holding anything back. Tears of pain or tears of joy; it doesn't matter. There's nothing more beautiful than your raw emotions. Just let yourSelf go there, and let others go there with you too. And when there's nothing to say but so much to feel, let yourSelf be embraced by Life – if it's through a loving hug, a loving smile, a beautiful sunset, a gentle breeze or simply by holding your own heart in the way you would hold a little child… with tenderness and care.

That is the language your heart speaks, and it's universal. It's the source that is within each and every one of us – the source of faith, the source of Love, the source of compassion and the source of forgiveness. In combination, all of these things are the source of very profound miracles, the main miracle being your own individual healing as a human being on the planet at this time; healing that brings **true** Love for yourSelf and all of Life.

Our emotional healing does involve going through periods of feeling grief, loss, sadness, heartbreak and heavy emotional states; it is a natural part of the process and it needs to be acknowledged. You must honor your heart and your deep healing. Whether the cause is something that occurred in your Life or simply the experience of painful emotions coming up to the surface, honoring your heart means that you give yourSelf the appropriate time and space to heal. Since your emotional state is tightly connected to your body, you might actually feel physical symptoms while moving through some sort of an emotional release or emotional healing. You might feel more tired with an increased need to sleep and rest. You might feel like you need to retreat for a period of time. That's all very normal during times of deep healing of the heart. When you get injured or hurt in some way and your body needs to heal, don't you usually need more resting time? Do you think that a broken heart or an emotional recovery is any different? Your emotional body can restore itself while you rest in the same way your physical body does.

The way of the heart teaches us to take care of our emotional body, which can feel like a complete foreign territory for many people, especially men. Living in a society that is so driven by external goals and achievements does a number on people's emotional well-being, resulting in a severe disconnection from one's heart and emotions. We can't have unattended wounds and a heart that is *fully* open at the same time – a piece of your heart will always remain shut until you attend to your pain by treating it with care and compassion rather than just pushing your way through it.

This new approach asks you to take care of your heart in the same way you take care of your body. By doing so, you'll be able to move through any emotional state more gracefully and with more ease. However, if you keep pushing it away or neglecting your emotional needs in times of pain or inner crisis, you'll keep the wound open and unattended instead of letting your heart do its healing.

THE POWER OF FORGIVENESS

We've all had our fair share of painful experiences, whether the source of hurt was a parent, a sibling, a lover, a partner, a friend and so forth. Although the memory may always live within us, it is our choice whether we want to carry any sense of resentment or blame for the rest of our lives. Carrying a sense of resentment toward anyone, regardless of who this person is, is one of the most toxic energies for your well-being and will keep the doors to the temple of your heart tightly shut. Forgiving someone doesn't mean forgetting and it doesn't mean you welcome them back into your Life (unless you want to of course, which can be a wonderful thing). Forgiveness means you have the ability to see them through the eyes of compassion knowing that this person or people did the best they could, even if that makes absolutely no sense to the mind. The way of the heart is not one of logic.

The most important piece about forgiveness is actually forgiving yourSelf first and foremost, which can be the hardest thing sometimes, right? Are you still beating yourSelf up for any past choices that were, let's say, less than ideal? Choices that put you in horrible situations or choices that cost you a great deal of your physical, mental or emotional well-being? Whether it be lifestyle choices, relationships choices, career choices, or simply the choice to not follow what your inner guidance was in fact telling you. Or maybe you've hurt somebody and were the catalyst for someone's heart break or pain...

Even though in retrospect you can recognize that wasn't your "best performance" and that you could have probably made a better choice, in truth, in that particular moment, that was the best you could have done. The fact of the matter is that everybody is doing the best they can with what they have, what they know, and their level of awareness, even if you think they (or you) can do better. The way of the heart accepts everyone, (and especially yourSelf) for who they are and the choices they make along the way.

Our ability to forgive ourselves and others, (whether others are people who are close to us or not), is a core theme in a heart-centered way of living. Although we can witness some atrocious behaviours, both on a personal level and definitely on the global stage, the truth is that we cannot control other people's actions; but we can choose the kind of energy with which we respond. Not only are forgiveness and compassion the heart's choices, but both will always be your ticket to true freedom. Feeling strong emotions like anger, sadness and even disgust toward certain behaviors or people is very natural, but turning these emotions into resentment or in some cases hatred, is extremely toxic. There are ways to work with these strong emotions without letting them fester within us to eventually turn into emotional poison.

It is important to note that most of the time these emotions are very much unconscious – hidden wounds that turn into lurking shadows within the dark corners of your emotional temple. You may not be walking around consciously feeling resentful toward someone or yourSelf, but if there are any unresolved emotional issues, there will most likely be some lurking shadows you're not aware of, shadows that play out as different emotional patterns you keep repeating while holding your heart hostage in the prison of resentment, guilt or shame. These emotional patterns can look like toxic relationships, unconscious hunger for emotional drama, the desire to save or to be saved by someone, codependency, jealousy, possessiveness and so forth.

No matter how emotionally intelligent and mature you may be, if there are *any* emotional wounds related to your mother or father (that's usually the biggest one), any feelings of abandonment, lack of nurturing or lack of Love, the same toxic patterns in your Life (especially in your relationships) will keep haunting you until you bring resolution to the core of the emotional issue. These emotional wounds go way back to your childhood, your time in the womb, time of conception and even past lives so we must be willing to face what is most likely lying dormant deep down in the unconscious. That is the bridge to your heart, the bridge between heaven and hell – hell being your shadows manifested as destructive patterns and heaven being the light of your awareness with its power to bring more understanding, more forgiveness, more compassion and more Love into your Life.

As part of your emotional healing and as you learn how to embrace the way of the heart more and more, if there's someone in your Life (whether yourSelf or someone else) who you still resent or blame, I invite you to make the choice to forgive that person right now at depth. Completely let it go knowing we all make mistakes. Choose to free yourSelf from the toxicity of any harsh emotions toward yourSelf and others. You can choose not to forget but you can certainly choose to forgive. This process of actively choosing forgiveness may take days, months or in some cases, years of practice. The pain might not disappear right away however, the conscious choice you're making to forgive and release, automatically puts things in motion and closes the loop of the same recurring emotional pain, allowing profound healing to occur within the temple of your heart.

There are different tools and practices which can assist you in the process of forgiving, even if you're not holding on to any conscious resentment. **All of us can benefit from practicing forgiving ourselves as an act of profound Self-Love and acceptance.** It took me awhile to be able to forgive mySelf for any harmful and unloving choices I've made along the way, either personally or with others. But once I shifted my perception of mySelf to one of unconditional Love, harsh feelings of guilt and judgment were replaced by compassion and understanding; and we can cultivate these feelings within us by practicing true forgiveness.

Asking for forgiveness doesn't imply guilt or blame. Even though some of our past choices weren't the greatest, there's no need to feel guilty about it and where other people are concerned, there's no need to blame anyone else for what has taken place. What's done is done and there's perfection in that as well, as painful, unfair or unjust it may seem to be. After all, there is a divine plan orchestrating all of Life and we each play our part. Our job is to move forward with grace, make better choices as we keep on growing, and pray that others will do the same.

Taking it a step further, on a deeper level, as an individual who is a part of the human race, each of us is a spokesperson for humanity as a whole; which means each of us can ask for forgiveness on the behalf of those who don't know what they're doing. If you deeply feel for the Earth, if you deeply feel for those who suffer the consequences of other people's lack of awareness and compassion, know that you can turn your forgiveness practice into a larger container, a container that can encompass all of humanity and our planet as the body of Life that it is. Believe it or not, that's how powerful one individual heart can be; especially when backed by a very clear and loving intention.

Forgiving yourSelf or other people:

> Whenever you find yourSelf in a heated place, whether you feel angry with someone or hurt by someone, if you want to release yourSelf from any resentment or toxic emotions toward that person, try this forgiveness practice:
>
> In your meditation, call in the person who you resent, feel angry toward or hurt by (whether it's yourSelf or someone else) and what it is you feel hurt by, mad or disappointed about. It is important you **let yourSelf feel all of it** since forgiveness is not to be used as a mean of suppression or denial of your true feelings; it's merely a tool to help you release emotional toxicity you might be carrying within you. You might feel all these emotions in your body which is very helpful for the healing process... It can feel like pain in your chest or uneasy feeling in your stomach. Observe whatever is coming up for you.
>
> After you've allowed yourSelf to feel your emotions and bring your pain to the surface (however big or small), start thinking about all the things you Love about them (or yourSelf), all the ways in which they bring you joy and support you. If you find ab-

solutely nothing you can think of (which is possible at times when there's a lot of pain or resentment), just acknowledge the valuable lessons you've learned from this person or the situation no matter how difficult it was. Recognize the gifts that have come from this relationship or from any specific situation. Once you're able to feel that sense of acknowledgment, even if it's the tiniest glimpse of it, go deeper into the feeling of that gratitude, acceptance, appreciation, maybe even Love. Stay in that sensation as long as you can and notice the difference in your body when you are immersed in that feeling as opposed to the feeling of resentment or anger you started with.

Let a sense of relief wash over you. The feeling of relief and release means you are letting go – that is forgiveness. Please remember that forgiveness is indeed a process, especially when we are dealing with deep wounds we are digging out of the unconscious. Whether you're working on forgiving yourSelf, other people or both, give yourSelf as much time as you need until you find true resolution within yourSelf. You'll know you have closed the loop when harsh emotions don't bubble up anymore and/or when old emotional and behavioral patterns disappear out of your Life.

If you are dealing with major emotional wounds, very strong emotions, or a great deal of resentment or guilt, try this practice for 30 days. By using this simple tool every day for a month (or more if you'd like to), you'll start letting this sense of relief really settle into your body and move through your heart as it clears away any debris of old pain and sorrow. It can be difficult to forgive yourSelf or someone else when there's a lot of regret, hurt or anger but it can be done by your willingness to let go of toxic emotions and open yourSelf up to more compassion and Love.

Asking to be forgiven – by yourSelf, other people and our planet

One of the most profound tools for this type of forgiveness process is an ancient Hawaiian prayer used for healing, transformation and increased inner-peace and Self-Love called Ho'oponopono. The literal translation of the name is "to make right again". It's a simple yet profound way to bring healing and forgiveness into your Life as it seeks to bring harmony, Love and balance into *all* of our relations. It was traditionally used to heal relationships between two or more people but it is also a powerful way to heal the relationship you have with yourSelf as much as it is a powerful tool to heal a relationship with another, to clear the energy of past hurts and traumas, and to heal our relationship with the Earth.

The beauty and value of this process is that it can be done face to face with another person or people or it can be done alone by you bringing that person into your mind's eye and into your heart. The same thing applies when directing this practice toward yourSelf or the planet as a whole. As with the practice above, this prayer can also be used when you're looking to find peace from a situation in which another person caused you pain and you're simply wanting to let go of any hard feelings and hurt as a way to bring more Love and compassion into your Life.

When doing it by yourSelf, whether the object of forgiveness is you, someone in your Life, or the planet as a whole, you can either sit in meditation or you can do it in bed before falling asleep. Ho'oponopono involves a simple mantra/prayer:

I Love you.
I'm sorry.
Please forgive me.
Thank you.

As you picture that person, your own Self or our planet, see yourSelf saying these words to that person or image over and over again… Repeat it as many times and for as long as you feel fit for you. This prayer is very helpful in situations where it is not possible to come face to face with another person for whatever reason. If the person is still alive but is too hurt to speak with you or see you, doing this practice for 30 days or longer, can bring about miracles. That's how impactful this prayer is when you set a very clear intention to heal your own heart first and thereby heal a relationship with another.

Even if you never hear from that person again, have faith in your heart that your prayer has indeed reached them which will allow them to go forward with greater Love and forgiveness in their heart. It is important to use this prayer for your own healing first and foremost, remembering that all of our hearts are essentially connected so your own healing spills over into other hearts; knowingly or not. Whether you seek to be forgiven, forgive someone, or are seeking Self-forgiveness, this mantra works for all situations. The words are a way of clearing energy for the person saying the prayer, no matter who's involved or what has taken place. This will remove the associated energies on your end and is a way of saying to yourSelf and the Universe, **"I no longer allow these dark and heavy energies to live in my body and in my heart."**

As you use this prayer on a consistent basis for as long as you need to, regardless of what's going to unfold in your relationships, the inner process you'll be experiencing will be the most profound one. You'll begin peeling back some of the deepest layers of your heart by releasing old and even ancient feelings of guilt, shame, remorse, hurt, and human suffering. This can be extremely cathartic and transformative if you allow yourSelf to just dive into it. Let each layer you peel be released with ease until you find a new and lighter energy to fill your heart and your Life. This may happen in an instant or it may take longer. The best way to move through this healing efficiently and gracefully is to expect nothing and be open to anything; **to be open and willing for your heart to take you on a journey of a Lifetime...**

Chapter 10

The Temple of your Soul – Spiritual Well-Being & Spiritual Integrity

"Asking ourselves 'Who am I?' is the first step to understanding who we've been since the beginning of time and who we'll be after we die." - *Alberto Villoldo, Ph.D.*

We can all agree that spirituality is a broad concept with room for many different perspectives. For me, spirituality, like the concept of God, isn't limited to religion. Religion does have a pure spiritual foundation and in their essence, all religions point to the same place. It is modern religion that has gotten all twisted up, turning away from what spirituality is actually about. Same thing applies to many 'new age' spiritual movements. Anything that is either very rigid and closed-minded, divides people, makes you feel powerless and small, or doesn't recognize the divinity in you *as* a human being, in my view, has nothing to do with *true* spirituality.

People are drawn to spirituality in the first place (or any type of a spiritual practice) because they search for meaning; it's a very natural urge that wakes something up inside of us. On some level, we all desire a sense of connection to the larger picture of Life which makes it a universal human experience and something that touches us all.

Within this search, and especially at a time when humanity is experiencing immense shifts, redefining spirituality is inevitable. The new generation of spirituality I'm here to co-create and be a part of is the kind of spirituality that doesn't separate human from spirit or physical matter from God. The kind of spirituality that opens one's eyes and heart to **see who they truly are – a soul in physical form with a unique individual expression**. It's time for a spiritual foundation that is based on merging our human body (and its animalistic nature) with the nature of spirit; form and formless coming together as one. There is a hunger for spiritual teachings that show us how to *truly* utilize our physical temple as an expression and an outlet for spirit; not the opposite.

We can no longer believe that spirituality is about transcending the body and our human nature nor can we continue to believe that God (spirit) is either something outside of ourselves or merely a fabricated concept. Any one of those beliefs are quite harmful to one's spiritual well-being and usually have physical, mental, and emotional implications as well. If you can't see that it's indeed a blessing to be born as a human and that God does reside within every cell of your being, all the spiritual practices in the world are not going to feed what your soul is really hungry for; and that is for you to recognize who you truly are. Once we embody this knowledge and *live as that*, we become a blessing to ourselves, our children, and the whole of humanity. After all, isn't that what spirituality is all about?

Your spiritual well-being is determined by your ability to experience the meaning and purpose of Life through the lens of Love and appreciation – loving all of yourSelf unconditionally and having true appreciation for your human experience. Spirituality and our spiritual practices are merely tools to help us establish a line of communication with our soul just so we can get in touch with our divine nature. When that line is open, your spiritual channel helps you purify anything that troubles your soul and holds you back from **living as a fully realized and embodied** human being.

Having a realization is not enough – *we must embody that which we have realized and integrate our wisdom into our choices and actions.* That is called spiritual integrity. Humans who are realized *and* integrated in that way, are human beings who function as their greatest potential, a potential that leads directly to true happiness, true abundance, unconditional Love, unwavering faith, and true liberation.

Moreover, a realized and integrated human being can translate their sense of connectedness with Life into their unique and creative expression; and your own individual, unique expression is a form of devotion. Your unique expression goes hand in hand with who you are as a soul. That expression can be art, music, dance, writing, cooking, teaching, singing, healing, gardening, building, acting, mentoring and so much more... Your unique expression can even be as simple as the way you choose to go about Life, a way that is unique and authentic to you. Giving your creative expression an outlet to flow through you is an *essential* part of your spiritual mission your soul is here to fulfill and plays a crucial role on your spiritual journey as a human being.

See yourSelf as a river... a flowing river. Each and every one of us is a river in the larger stream of Life and each river has its unique flow and rhythm.

And just like all rivers go back to the same ocean they are made of, all of us as individuals are essentially connected to the same source; we are not separate from it, we are just making our way to unite with it once again. And the journey is **internal**. The flow of Life we're here to experience is an 'inside flow.'; it always starts from within.

This 'inside flow', when flowing rather than stagnant, is an indication of your spiritual well-being. When it is indeed flowing, you move about your Life with a sense of what seems to be a power greater than yourSelf. That sense comes from your ability to tap into your greatest potential, your highest and greatest version of yourSelf. Just like the river and the ocean, although they seem separate, they are both made out of the same water. You and I are made out of the same essence of God; that power we perceive as greater than ourselves. The spiritual journey of each human river is to re-unite with that source *through* our human experience and not apart from it.

What can you experience when your spiritual channel is clear and your internal flow is free from obstructions?

- You know who you are beyond your persona – you are aware of the larger context of your existence.
- You know that you are loved and cared for by God (Life) even when things may appear difficult on the surface.
- You see Life and your human experience as a gift.
- You feel fulfilled and satisfied with Life regardless of external circumstances (and if you're not, you know what to do in order to achieve a sense of fulfillment).
- You have a meaningful relationship with yourSelf and with Life as a whole.

- You feel your inner strength carrying you through Life, knowing you are supported by God. That sense of inner knowing gives you tremendous courage to live your Life according to your own personal truth and guidance.
- You feel confidant about where you're at in Life presently, where you're going in the future (even if the future is a mystery), and you don't hold any resentments regarding the past.
- You trust in the divine plan that God has for you and everyone else.

For reasons beyond my comprehension, it seems like forgetting all of the above every once in awhile comes as a package deal with our human experience. Maybe this is because part of the deal is to learn how to remember, to learn how to keep the river flowing as we make our way back to the ocean. We experience this state of amnesia when we enter into the zone of our ego's limited perspective from inside the valley instead of looking at Life from the mountain top where our soul resides. And there's nothing wrong with that. If anything, once we get a glimpse of the mountain top view and experience true liberation and inner joy, we recognize how valuable it is and therefore **dedicate time and energy** to cultivate that state as much as possible. Those glimpses give you a clear sense of Life's deeper meaning, the deeper purpose of your own existence as a unique soul, and a deeper understanding of the interconnectivity of this entire creation.

DO YOU HAVE A SPIRITUAL ANCHOR?
Your spiritual practice

Is it possible to live in a state of remembrance all the time? Is it possible to remain standing on the mountain top, seeing Life from our soul's perspective without the need to take occasional trips to the valley of our ego's limited point of view? Maybe yes, maybe not. What I can tell you from my own experience is that the spiritual journey involves oscillating between the two just so we can build our **spiritual endurance**. The more endurance we develop, the more natural it feels to climb up and stay at the top in high elevation. If you were to undertake a physical training, wouldn't you build your endurance and stamina over time by climbing a tall mountain in high elevation on a consistent basis? Wouldn't you improve your breath capacity and ability to sustain your energy? Wouldn't it get easier with practice?

Well, the same thing applies to the kind of spiritual endurance you need to have on this journey as you learn how to master your Life. The more trips you take up to the mountain top, the better it gets and the longer you're able to stay up there. The more at home you feel up top, the less frequent are your visits back down to the valley of your ego.

Building your spiritual endurance gives you the ability to function well (if not better) in higher elevation without feeling like it's too much. As surprising as it may sound, that can be the biggest challenge for some. As humans, we get glimpses of how it feels to be living from an expanded state of awareness, glimpses of the joy and true fulfillment that come from living as one with our soul, and we freak out. It feels too much and isn't always easy. So we dip back down to the narrow view of our ego's limited perspective and choices. It's a safe place for many, a place where the air is not so thin. But, once we develop our endurance and the necessary skills we need to embark on this excursion, we don't only in-joy the climb (even when it's challenging) but we feel ready and well equipped to set up camp at the mountain top. Over time and with our loving dedication, we eventually get acclimated to the same conditions that felt very uncomfortable and scary at first.

So how do we build this endurance in the most beneficial way? How do we build it without exhausting ourselves? How do we sustain our energy at the top, minimizing and even avoiding our trips back down? How do we maintain our breath at the top in order to in-joy the view instead of freaking out? For all these valuable skills you need a solid anchor. A spiritual anchor. Something that guides, helps, and encourages you to stick with it when it gets challenging; when it's tempting to run down the slope and back into the safety of the valley. Something that reminds you who you are when you think there's absolutely nothing left in you. *It is your spiritual personal trainer who can see you as a soul when you forget.*

And yes, that someone is you. It is an inside job in which you are asked to established this anchor and find your inner spiritual personal trainer who is in direct communication with your soul on a regular basis.

Having a spiritual practice can be that powerful anchor, a tool to help us live in a state of remembrance. Our spiritual practice acts as the anchor we need in order to sustain our energy, no matter how high the mountain we're climbing; and it helps us keep that line of communication with our soul open and clear. For me, yoga and meditation were the foundation for my anchor; and they still are. I personally in-joy these practices (which I'll cover) and believe them to be essential on our Life journey. However, a spiritual practice is definitely not limited to one aspect and can be expressed as your creativity, your work-out, the dance floor, your music, surfing the waves in the ocean, snowboarding, making food, making Love, being in nature and so forth. As with the concept of spirituality, what we refer to as spiritual practice has room for many different interpretations as well.

In my view, spiritual practice is simply anything that gets you in touch with your true nature; with your soul. With that which you describe as God – the flow of Life within and around you. Anything that gets you out of your thinking mind and into the present moment; into your body and loving heart. Anything that helps you dive into the innermost aspects of yourSelf to see that the entire universe lives inside of you; always has and always will. Whatever it is that makes you feel like you're standing on the mountain top with a clear seeing of the entire view. Any practices that invigorates not only your body, but your heart and soul, connecting you deeper to the exquisite beauty of Life. And who *you* truly are.

Now, the trick with any spiritual practice is the ability to take it from that space and into your day to day Life. That's where it gets tricky. It's easy to connect to the vastness of your soul's view in your meditation, on your yoga mat, in your art studio, on your surfboard, in bed with your lover or in the middle of a lush forest. But what about everywhere else? What about times when you need to make important (and sometimes hard) choices in Life – can you still be connected to the vastness of your soul's view? When things do get challenging or overwhelming, do you still know in your heart that Life has your back? When walking down the street, are you able to recognize that it's indeed the entire universe dressed as you doing the walking? And when interacting with another, are you still able to recognize the divine nature of both of you or did you leave that part on your yoga mat?

When we live as our spiritual practice as opposed to having our spiritual practice be something we do on the side, the experience of ourselves and of Life goes to a whole other level; and that's what we call *embodiment* – embodying the wisdom of our spiritual connection. From that place we are able to not only pray to God, but **to live as God**. Living in that way becomes accessible when you know you are a divine soul wearing a human costume; no small thing indeed. But when we develop a strong spiritual anchor, we increase our ability to experience Life from our soul's point of view; and nothing makes your soul more satisfied than that.

Whatever works best for you at this time in your Life, I encourage you to adopt some sort of a daily practice that is rooted in your connection to source; call it a spiritual practice or not, make it a regular habit to plug your human battery into the charger of spirit every day. Don't use your spiritual practice only at times of need but rather, make it an active part of your Life no matter how big or small. After all, it's the things we do daily which make the biggest difference in the long run.

What would happen if you only brushed your teeth twice a week? Or showered twice a month? Think in these terms in regards to your spiritual practice. Your spiritual practice is a time you carve for yourSelf to commune with the God within you, to plug your human battery into the divine source of creation. It's definitely an act of Self-Love since it plays an integral role in your overall state of well-being.

I would like to mention some of the more traditional spiritual practices we are familiar with and hopefully inspire you to give it a shot if it's new to you, to deepen your practice if you've already been doing it for a while, or perhaps reconnect in a new way to a practice you used to have. Any of the following practices are big contributors to an elevated, expanded, peaceful, and vibrant state of well-being that is Self-generated and truly fulfilling.

These different practices have helped me open my body, open my heart, quiet my mind and most importantly, find my way back home; back to my soul. The practice itself isn't the end result, it's merely a helper on the journey. The practice gives your spiritual anchor the necessary weight and strength to keep you rooted in the center of your soul; even in the midst of a complete storm.

Meditation

Your meditation practice can be as simple or as elaborate as you'd like it to be; as short or as long. Make it your own and make it work for you. There are various meditation practices to choose from so find what works best for you; different methods will work at different times. As I've mentioned, regardless of what is your prefered method of meditation, making everything a meditation is ultimately what the practice of meditation is pointing us toward – to bring mindfulness into our moment to moment, day to day Life. The practice of meditation not only helps us remember our divine nature but also induces feelings of calm and clear-headedness, improves concentration and attention, and makes us more productive and efficient with our time.

Meditating for 10 minutes a day is infinitely better than meditating for an hour once a week. Even if you can only sit and meditate for a few minutes, make it a daily thing rather than a scattered or inconsistent practice.

If meditation is new to you, start small. You'll get frustrated and discouraged if you try to meditate for longer periods of time if you're not used to it. Start with 5 or 10 minutes and increase that time as you go. It's ok if your mind wanders. Just notice it at first, then **gently** guide your mind back to the present moment; gently being the operative word. Be easy on yourSelf. No need to get frustrated regardless of how long you've had a meditation practice. Your meditations will actually become much more productive when you gently bring your attention back rather than being overly militant with yourSelf.

Yoga

The practice of yoga is a centuries-old spiritual practice that aims to *create a sense of union* within the practitioner. The meaning of the word Yoga is union and the practice itself helps us find that state of union within ourselves – mind and heart, body and soul, feminine and masculine. Yoga teaches us balance and grace and is a phenomenal way to get into your body and out of your head (especially if you spend a lot of time in that neighbourhood). The practice of yoga focuses on physical postures, breath, mindfulness, and ethical behaviors. The systematic practice of yoga has been found to reduce inflammation and stress, regulate blood pressure, decrease depression and anxiety, and increase feelings of well-being.

As with your meditation practice, there are numerous styles of yoga to choose from and you'll discover that each style has a different flavor. Choose your favorite flavor (which might change over time) and be as consistent as possible with your practice. You don't need to be flexible to start a yoga practice. Many people are intimidated by the practice of yoga and are afraid to try it because they think they are lacking the necessary flexibility. Well, first of all, that's probably a good reason to start a yoga practice, allowing the body to open and become limber. Second, *the true core essence of yoga is beyond the fancy physical postures we see out there.* It is the spiritual and philosophical aspect of this tradition which has the ability (through the physical practice) to get you more in touch with your Godly nature and to guide you back home to your true Self.

Prayer

For those who believe, the power of prayer is extremely impactful and can help us heal our heart, connect with our soul, and send out our Love and good intentions to others and the world. Prayer has the power to induce relaxation, along with the feelings of faith, gratitude, and compassion – all of which have a very positive effect on your overall well-being. There are different types of prayer, and of course, there isn't one specific way to do it. How you choose to pray and communicate with God and your soul is up to you. It may look like a traditional prayer or it might be something you make up yourSelf. What's important is your intention behind it and your level of faith – faith in a higher power and in your soul to guide you in the highest direction.

This belief alone can provide a sense of comfort and support in difficult times which increases our ability to trust Life and be at ease with the divine plan (especially when the divine plan doesn't match our personal plans). The more you pray and strengthen your connection to the source of all of creation, the more you align with your soul and the highest road for your Life. The force of internal and external resistance (that sense of kicking and screaming) will start to dissipate and eventually vanish when you are living in harmony with the higher purpose your soul has in store for you.

You may choose to pray every day or less frequently and the way in which you pray may differ each time. However you choose to go about it, always express your Love and gratitude to God, to Life, and to yourSelf at the end of your prayer and ask to gracefully align your will with the divine will. You can begin your prayer by taking a few deep breaths, relaxing into your body. Allow any strains to melt away with each breath, breathing in relaxation, exhaling out any residual stress. Feel yourSelf entering into a place of Love, a place where God hears and feels everything you have to say. Become present to what's coming up for you and pray from your heart rather than your mind; no need to think about your prayer, just let it out unedited.

Here's a simple prayer you can use if you're not sure where to begin:

> *May I be at peace.*
> *May my heart remain open to Love.*
> *May I awaken to the light and truth of my own true nature.*
> *May I be a source of healing and inspiration for all beings.*
> *And so it is.*
> *Thank you, Thank you, Thank you.*

SPIRITUAL INTEGRITY

Integrity stems from the Latin word 'integer' which means whole and complete. Integrity requires an inner sense of wholeness and consistency of character. When we live in integrity, we align our thoughts, words, choices, decisions, methods, and actions; in other words, there's congruency between all these aspects. Spiritual integrity calls you to match all these aspects with your soul and the highest road for your Life. Now, if there's a higher road for your Life, what would be the opposite of that? Let us answer that question by looking at the following: Have you ever made a choice or a decision in your Life based on any of these factors?

- Fear of changing the status quo of your Life (although your intuition was screaming at you)

- Fearing the uncertainty of the future
- A desire for immediate gratification (although you *knew* it wasn't the best choice)
- A need to maintain a certain reputation or be perceived in a certain way
- A need to please someone else (even though it's against your truth)
- A need to control a situation (or someone else)
- A need to make a point
- A desire to "get even" with someone

There's more we can add to the list but I believe you get the point. Developing spiritual integrity helps us align our higher wisdom with day-to-day living; to bring our spiritual knowledge and realizations into every aspect of Life. To close the gap between the mountain top and the valley – your soul and your ego; until there's no gap left. But we must know ourselves as a soul before we can bring the two together. By developing a loving relationship with yourSelf and with God, and by understanding the nature of your ego vs. your soul, you are that much more equipped to recognize the gap, the root cause of the gap, and what needs to be done in order to close it for good.

When your soul and your ego still operate within you as opponents rather than best friends, you experience conflicting desires and agendas for your Life – you know what is the highest road to take yet you feel compelled to act differently. Even though you can see clearly from the mountain top of your soul which paths will lead you to where you want to go and which won't, you choose your path as if you were still blindly walking through the valley of your ego. Whether it's based on fear, egoic desires, or emotional wounding, making choices that go against what you know is true or healthy for you is out of integrity with yourSelf. When soul and ego reunite again (because ultimately they're not two separate things, they just appear to be – like the river and the ocean), you experience yourSelf as an integrated human being.

An integrated human being has greater ability to have spiritual integrity. When our spiritual integrity is intact, we truly start seeing **everything** as God without exceptions – the physical is not less Godly than the spiritual and our dark shadows are not less divine than our light. It is indeed our Godly mission (as part of our divine purpose) to learn how to live within the duality of this reality without rejecting any of it but instead, Love it, work with it, and master it. If you hold a belief that spiritual Life is all about light where darkness doesn't exist, well, I have news for you... When it comes to this Earth plane we are occupying as human beings, like it or not, both light and dark exist; yes, within each and every one of us. We must integrate both into the totality of who we are since *full integration is a prerequisite to attaining spiritual integrity.*

We ALL have the same operating system with the same light and dark functions. Our light function is our expansive awareness and our ability to make choices based on that awareness while our dark function is our hidden shadows; the very same shadows that cause us to make choices based on unconscious wounds. How can one have spiritual integrity when actions are still driven by hidden shadows? One has to first acknowledge (and most importantly, embrace) their shadows to then start integrating these pieces into the totality of who they are. The slightest aversion, suppression or denial leads to separation within oneSelf. That separation is a result of rejecting something that is inherently natural – the fact that we all carry both light and dark. The more one perpetuates a state of separation within themselves, the less integrated they are which leads to the widening of the gap; and we're looking to close it.

The mastery lies in the ability to work with your shadows and turn your shadows into light; to become your own alchemist. That becomes available when you've integrated both aspects of yourSelf. When your shadows become a source of power as a result of shining the light of your awareness onto them, true spiritual integrity takes place. When everything clicks in together – your thoughts, words, choices, actions *and* your soul's highest truth and wisdom, you get to live and bring forth more of your soul's essence; the truth of who you are, as opposed to playing any roles which are far off from the highest road for your Life. Far from the direction of your greatest potential, fullest expression and truest purpose. And that is all part of the promise you made to God before your birth; and by you I mean your soul. Your soul joyously accepted to play the role of you and it's up to you whether you're going to fulfill that promise, how you choose to go about it, and what it is you choose to bring forth.

"If you bring forth what is within you, what you bring forth will save you. If you do not bring forth what is within you, what you do not bring forth will destroy you." - *Jesus Christ*

Creating Spiritual Integrity in Life

Choose to take right action – Before taking action, consider your options and determine what feels right to you. Does your body tense up or relax when considering your next move? Is it in your highest good and the highest good of those around you? Is it aligned with your personal and spiritual morals? Does it bring harm to yourSelf or another or does it help? Choose your actions from a place of being in high service to the divine plan even when that plan may not match your personal agenda or desire.

Walk the talk – Do you indeed practice and embody what you preach? Are you living in accordance with your spiritual wisdom? Especially if you are a coach, a teacher, a healer or a guide for others, do you take your own advice? Are you a shining example of all that you know and guide people to? Walking your own talk is essential to living Life of spiritual integrity; and that can only be attained through a process of personal integration.

Clear yourSelf energetically – Get rid of negativity on a regular basis and embrace inner peace. If there is a circumstance taking you off center that is out of your control, do the best you can to move through and release any extraneous anxiety. That's where a spiritual practice comes in handy. Instead of accumulating negativity and anxieties (which can happen easily if you don't pay attention), you can lighten your load by clearing your energy field, moving your body, grounding yourSelf by being in nature, or any other methods that help you remove toxicity and stress. The more often you do this, the less chances negativity will stick to you.

Take responsibility – Own the decisions you make and the actions you take and look for the lessons in every experience. Understand your role in the situation and what better choices can be made going forward. Don't be a victim by blaming others for your circumstances. Take appropriate action to move past the issue and communicate with others in a clear and honest way without pointing fingers.

Constant connection to God – Whether you carve a specific time for your spiritual practice or not, remain open and listen to divine guidance. You can start your day with the intent of doing so, increasing your ability to stay in constant communion with the source of creation. The more you follow this divine guidance (no matter how irrational it may be or how much it opposes your ego's desires), the stronger and more consistent the connection becomes.

Continuous expansion – Know that your evolution as a soul is not only natural but needed so encourage yourSelf to evolve on a regular basis. Avoid stagnation and seek opportunities to express your true nature in new ways as you feel guided. Make Life your classroom and see every situation as an opportunity for you to learn and evolve.

Accept not judge – Just like all rivers flow back to the same ocean, all paths lead to the same source. Our differences enrich the world so no need to pass judgments on other people's chosen path. You can disagree with certain paths, but understand that each person is here on their own individual journey, and we each have our personal lessons to learn. Accept their way as much as yours, allowing everyone to make the choices they feel are best for them.

Live in gratitude – Appreciate and learn to see the blessing for everything in your Life, even when it appears to be negative at first. It is there for a reason as part of the divine plan to which we are all learning to open our minds and hearts. Your soul seeks to grow so even when you don't like it, know it's playing an important part in your own evolution; after a while, there won't be much resistance left in you.

Chapter 11

Your external world – how does it affect you?

As with anything else in your Life, make your external world be something that supports and enhances your well-being. Anything in your external reality that is a source of either stress, heaviness, stagnation or complication and is compromising your well-being in any way, needs to be recognized for what it is and be addressed as soon as possible. There are times when minor adjustments can be enough in order to bring more harmony but in some cases, bigger adjustments are needed which do require a complete 180.

CLEARING, SIMPLIFYING & ORGANIZING YOUR PHYSICAL SPACE

Keeping the space around you tidy and clean is crucial for your overall well-being. There's an energetic exchange that happens between you and any space you spend time in – whether it's your home, your office, or your car. If your personal space is messy, cluttered, disorganized, chaotic or dirty, how do you think that's going to affect you? What kind of an exchange happens under these conditions? In the same way that a cluttered and dirty internal environment affects your well-being, an external environment of that nature has it's own implications. It may be more subtle but nevertheless, it's there. Keep the spaces you spend time in (especially your home) as nurturing and pleasant as possible, turning your physical space into an external temple to support your inner temple.

Notice how a clean and organized space makes you feel as opposed to one that is cluttered and messy. Which one imparts more relaxation and peace and which one imparts tension and uneasy feeling? And who knows, maybe you like chaos and operate well under these conditions; I know many people who do. But I've also noticed how stressed out those individuals usually are since there's some sort of internal chaos accompanying the external one. Experiment with treating all of your physical environments as little temples, spaces you can walk into and immediately feel at peace. Spaces in which you feel like the energy is flowing smoothly and harmoniously and as a result, support that same state within you.

The process of organizing and decluttering your external environment in order to create more space in your Life, physically and energetically, requires us to look at one of the number one things us humans like to accumulate: *Stuff*. How much stuff do you have? How much of it do you really need? Do you keep collecting more and more? Buying more and more? When was the last time you went through all that you own and sorted out what is needed and what isn't?

Taking inventory of your physical possessions will not only do wonders to your physical environment, but will also affect your overall state of well-being. Adding more and more stuff on top of what you already have is equivalent to consuming more food well after you feel full. At the end of the day, over-consumption is over-consumption whether it be food, stuff or anything in between. When we add more than we need (or can handle), we automatically make our Life more congested. Clutter, either physical, mental or emotional constricts the natural flow of Life and since everything is connected, even the most subtle things can impact your Life; positively or not.

Just for a moment, feel the word CLUTTER in your body... Try taking a deep breath while imagining clutter. Is there any ease there? Any room to take a full, refreshing breath? If the answer is no, you know there are no benefits to overconsumption or a cluttered state. There might even be an underlying feeling of stress when you are surrounded by extra stuff. If you're looking to create a sense of lightness in your Life, maybe to release what feels like 'stuck' energy, examine your physical environment and the amount of stuff you have accumulated throughout the years. How much of it do you use and how much of it do you really need or even want?

That can be stuff, but also any other physical possessions you own – clothes, investments, real estate, business deals, financial ties and the like. Simplify your physical reality by decluttering and organizing your Life, releasing what is not needed or wanted anymore. Let the following question guide you:

What do I need to do in order to simplify my reality and create more spaciousness in my Life?

ENERGY LEAKS

Energy leaks can show up very subtly and therefore require your accute awareness – like finding the almost invisible holes in the water bucket; you can barely see them but you know they're there. Sealing any energy leaks and **condensing your energy** will turn your Life force into a powerful laser beam, becoming **exponentially more efficient.** Your physical environment, when cluttered and chaotic can become an energy leak, but an energy leak can be anything that drains your energy, whether it's physical or not. Anything you choose to invest your time, energy, and money in can become an energy drain if it's out of balance and doesn't enhance your Life for the better. Those things can be:

• Lifestyle choices and different activities you choose to engage in
• People you choose to spend time with and surround yourSelf with
• Social obligations
• Your relationships
• Your job
• Your finances

Anything from the categories above that makes your Life either more complicated, overwhelming, stressful, or scattered can become an energy drain; so take note of that. Your Life can be full just make sure you fill it up with the right things, the right people, and the right activities. When driven by Self-Love and Self-worth, you will start valuing your time and energy that much more which will motivate you to create the most conducive and supportive environments for you to flourish and thrive in.

Now, of course, sometimes there are situations which can make our reality more full or stressful for a period of time. We do encounter challenges from time to time which may feel overwhelming, perhaps even chaotic; that is only natural and unavoidable. However, we can avoid the potential energy drain by *becoming uber efficient with the way we handle stress and chaos.* It is within our power to avoid any additional overwhelm when facing challenging situations in Life and our wise choices can help us navigate our way through it all in the most conducive manner.

Even the most seemingly complicated or overwhelming situation can become simple and less draining with the right approach and mindset. When guided by simplicity and ease, your driving force is finding solutions rather than focusing on the problems. The latter will always make things more complicated and will turn into a big energy drain. You can choose to turn a small flame into a blazing fire or conversely, choose to efficiently put that little flame to rest. You are also capable of turning the wildest blazing fire into a tiny flame if you strive to make Life simpler rather than the opposite. This mindset will help you see what is the best approach to take in any given situation which will keep your energy from leaking into the wrong places.

Solution oriented approach fuels your energy while problem oriented approach sucks your energy dry.

Some people may want to make things bigger and more complicated than they are or insist on focusing on the problem rather than the solution; but that doesn't mean you need to get sucked into it. The more you make simplicity your attitude of choice, the more you'll be able to observe all the unnecessary stuff humans choose to deal with (either physically, mentally or emotionally). So much of that drains our energy and precious resources while a much simpler path awaits our arrival.

Let the following questions guide you:

Are there any energetic drains in my Life and if so, where do they originate from? What can I do in order to condense my energy?

YOUR RELATIONSHIPS

Our relationships play an integral role in our lives. It is an essential part of our human experience and like any other part of our external world, it can either enhance or undermine the quality of Life and well-being. The people you choose to be close with are a direct reflection of your relationship with yourSelf – *all of your relationships and the quality of those relationships stem from your personal sense of Self-worth and Self-Love.* When you truly value and Love yourSelf, you will not tolerate **any** relationship that doesn't reflect that back to you. When your sense of Self-worth is in the right place, you will surround yourSelf only with those who truly see you, honor you, accept you, uplift you, respect your choices, and Love you for who you are. When committed to your overall well-being, you will form relationships that truly resonate with you, not just on the surface, but deeply within your heart and soul. Your sense of Self-worth will determine the kind of people you choose to be in relationship with and will also help you discern if and when it's time to let a relationship go...

Who you choose as your friends, as a partner, and as your community must feel in complete resonance with who you are. Surround yourSelf only with those who celebrate you as an individual and don't try to mould you into something you're not. Those who see you for who you are and help you cultivate your natural gifts and talents. Those who accept you and Love you unconditionally. Those who want what's best for you according to *your* personal guidance, not theirs. Within your relationships, you want to feel supported, understood, seen, and embraced... you want to feel like you can really grow into the best version of yourSelf... you want to feel like you can fully express yourSelf without inhibitions or fears... you want to feel like you can be authentic without hiding. If a relationship of any kind doesn't help you shine or even worst, tries to diminish your light, there's nothing for you there anymore. Don't be afraid to let go because I promise you, God has something so much better for you.

We either grow together or grow apart...

Choosing to maintain a relationship that is way overdue doesn't serve anyone involved, especially you. Staying in a relationship that doesn't fit a new version of yourSelf, is like trying to squeeze your foot into a tight shoe; if it's not a fit, why force it? Just like certain shoes and clothes don't fit you anymore either because your body changes or simply because your taste of fashion changes, so are the people in your Life. An old friend may or may not fit into who you are twenty years later. A partnership you've had with someone may not be the healthiest thing for you anymore; or the most fulfilling. What are you going to do? I'm not saying it's an easy step to take, but it's important to recognize which relationships feel harmonious and which don't.

When you stay in any relationship, even though your heart and soul are guiding you in a different direction, you turn your back on *yourSelf*; and that is disrespectful to YOU. When it comes to your relationships, (just like with anything else I cover in this book), your number one commitment is to yourSelf. That means you can't keep yourSelf a prisoner in any relationship just because you may feel one of the following:

- You feel bad about ending it (whatever the nature of the relationship is)
- You feel guilty about your true feelings regarding the relationship
- You are scared of the outcome
- You feel dependent on the other person (financially, emotionally or anything else)

- You worry about how other people are going to be affected by your decision

There's a difference between what is a healthy challenge to overcome in your relationship with another (since relationships do go through phases), and what is a clear turning point. As a function of Self-Love, you will know how to decipher between the two, recognizing when in fact, a relationships doesn't fit who you are anymore. If you're afraid to take a step in a new direction, that same Love for yourSelf will also provide you with all the courage you need.

It is not your job to change anyone or try to mould someone into something they're not. You as well don't need to pretend to be something you're not just to make a relationship work. There's a fine line between making healthy comprises in relationships and compromising who you are. When guided by your unwavering commitment to yourSelf, you will be driven to establish the healthiest, most balanced, most supportive, most nurturing, and most cohesive relationships in your Life; truly fulfilling relationships that are based on healthy interdependency rather than toxic co-dependency.

Healthy relationships - from co-dependency to interdependency

The topic of co-dependency and interdependency in relationships is extremely vast. Within the context of this book, as it relates to mastering your Life, I'm going to just touch on this subject a little bit since our relationships play **such** a significant role in our external world. Moreover, relationships and the ability to maintain healthy ones, is indeed something many of us are challenged with.

When a person forms a realtionship with another person (especially a close relationship), they immediately develop a level of dependency; which is absolutely fine. We see different levels of dependency in nature just as much as we see it between humans since it is a natural part of Life – plants and animals must coexist to survive. They depend upon each other because each provides something the other needs. Trees provide shade, a place to live, and food for nourishment while animals spread the seeds of plants and help with pollination. Those are examples of healthy dependency, also known as interdependency which is at the core of every healthy relationship. So what is the difference between interdependency and co-dependency? When does the line gets crossed from healthy dependency to an unhealthy one?

An interdependent relationship requires two people (or more) to be *autonomous* while being committed to the relationship. Being autonomous is the ability to function independently and authentically, despite the fact that you're in a relationship with someone or a part of a larger group. You don't lose your own individuality in the relationship and you don't look for others to complete you or fulfill you in any way, no matter how much your lives are intertwined.

What allows individuals to operate in this way is their level of Self-esteem and Self-worth. When you have healthy Self-esteem and *Self-generated confidence*, you are able to manage and be responsible for your own thoughts and emotions without needing to control someone else in order to feel good about yourSelf. When a relationship is based on interdependency and therefore is balanced and healthy, each individual shares power equally and takes responsibility for their own thoughts, emotions, actions, and contributions to the relationship; there's no blame or pointing fingers.

In a healthy relationship, differences are allowed and each person's individuality and independence is honored and celebrated. Under these conditions, individuals can be fully honest and transparent with one another. You are then able to listen to another person's feelings and needs without feeling guilty or becoming defensive; and you will also be received in the same way by the other person. When individuals are truly confident and their Self-esteem doesn't depend on other people (not even your closest partner), independence doesn't threaten the relationship anymore. In fact, the relationship can actually become a container for more freedom since it's based on mutual respect and support for each person's Life journey. All parties involved are committed to the highest road for their Life and the highest road of the relationship. It is indeed a much more of a heart centered approach to relationships, providing more nurturing and freedom as opposed to an ego driven approach which is seeking to hold on, to control, and to gratify egoic desires.

In unhealthy relationships based on co-dependency, individuals relate to one another in toxic ways, usually perpetuating patterns of obsession, Self-sacrifice, blame, dysfunctional communication, and the biggest one of all, control. Needless to say, all those patterns are both Self-destructive and hurtful to others and in some cases, can turn to be abusive either mentally, emotionally and in extreme cases, physically. I must say here that there are different levels as to how co-dependency may show up in your relationships – It can be very subtle in some cases but that doesn't mean it's not there. *We must pay attention to even the most subtle expressions.* There are prevalent imbalances in co-dependent relationships with struggles for power and control and a lack of personal responsibility. The impulse to control comes from an unconscious desire to make other people responsible for one's own fulfillment which brings about resentment and blame if those needs are not met. Within a relationship of that nature, individuals often feel either resentful or guilty because they feel responsible for the other person's feelings and moods.

You know you are in a co-dependent territory when there's no respect for each other's individuality and authenticity, and disagreements quickly turn into a blame game without taking any personal responsibility whatsoever. One of the most toxic patterns in co-dependent relationships is that despite the dysfunction and the pain that comes with it, individuals may feel trapped in the relationship because they believe they cannot function on their own; they become paralyzed by fear. A deep sense of insecurity can keep individuals in the most unhealthy relationships, believing that the other person (or people) are vital for their own sense of wholeness, Self-worth, and sense of security – either emotional, physical or both. In that case, independance becomes a threat to the relationship, causing the relationship to unknowingly act as a prison for the individual's true freedom and growth.

Can you look at some of your past relationships (or maybe even current ones) and recognize unhealthy patterns of codependency, as subtle as they may be? Whether it is you who feel insecure, the other person, or both. Having an insatiable hunger for emotional security and validation from other people (because we don't give that to ourselves), will never work. We will continue to experience some level of co-dependency in our relationships if we expect external sources to give us a sense of emotional security. As long as your sweet little ego sits in the dark, it will continue to run the show on your behalf, causing you to manage your relationships with an underlying sense of fear and control. So even though all you desire is to bring an open heart to the table, your unmet ego desires will interfere with that endeavor.

Relationships that are based on ego desires will always have a sour flavor of *'I need something from you.' 'I need a sense of control to make sure I get my needs met by you.'* When all of that is happening underneath the surface, the need for relationships can very easily turn into an addiction just like anything else – depending on an external source to fill us up. It is indeed an unending cycle. Your relationships will be so much healthier, more balanced, and more harmonious when all parties involved don't NEED the other person to fill them up. We then enhance one another rather than using each other unconsciously to try and fulfill a void that can only be fulfilled by oneSelf.

If you are full and complete within yourSelf, when you know how to be your own parent, best friend and companion for Life, you don't look for your relationships to provide you with that. It's not that we don't want or need relationships, it's just that we stop looking for other people to provide us with that which we can only give ourselves (That can be a friend, a lover, a spouse or anyone you form a close relationship with). When we heal our unconscious wounds with our **own personal loving embrace**, two (or more) individuals can then come together from a fulfilled place, automatically setting up the stage for a much stronger and healthier relationship.

Whatever the nature of the relationship is, when it is formed by individuals who are full of their own Love, that relationship becomes a container for individuals to thrive and grow together instead of being a feeding ground for unconscious shadows and unresolved emotional wounds. These kind of relationships are the ones we want to cultivate more in our lives as part of humanity's evolution and a new world foundation based on empowered, aware, mindful, integrated, and loving individuals. As the building blocks of humanity, the way we come together and form relationships, families, communities, and societies, will determine how much we can evolve and flourish as a whole; it really is up to every single one of us.

Closing words

As you've learned through this book, the foundation for your new and upgraded Life and state of well-being is indeed your relationship with yourSelf; your ability to put Self-Love into action on a regular basis. Committing to loving yourSelf like you never have before will be your guide to keep you on track. I said it at the beginning and I'll say it again: *This is not about perfection, it's about practice.* You fall off the horse just so you can practice getting back up; but you pick yourSelf back up with Love and compassion. Over time, as you'll continue to expand your capacity to Love and embrace yourSelf, there will be less and less "falls". The only force that will be guiding your choices will be Love and only Love.

Don't limit what is possible for your Life or how wonderful it can be. Stay committed to your well-being and yourSelf; everything in your Life will continue to be upgraded as a result. This is the beginning of a beautiful chapter, a chapter that is dedicated to mastering your Life by learning how to take care of yourSelf, how to deepen your relationship with yourSelf, and how to rise in Love again, and again, and again.

IN-JOY THE RIDE...

Be authentically you. Never be afraid to express your brilliance. You are a pillar of light who can create ripples upon ripples of positive impact.

You are a change agent. That's why you are here.

And you know that the change begins with you.

You are not afraid to jump.

Not afraid to shine.

Not afraid to Love.

Not afraid to live as the BEST version of yourSelf.

There is no other way because the only way out is by going in.

You are the one you've been waiting for.

No need to wait any longer.

Let the struggle end.

Be the change and Master your Life with Love.

Because one by one we are elevating humanity and creating a better world.

Our time has come.

Additional resources and support

There are many practical tools in this book which are for you to use as you please. However, If you would like to have a well-rounded and comprehensive launching ground, I recommend you look into my complimentary guide to this book – *40 Days to Self-Mastery* (available for purchase as an ebook - on my website). It is a 40-day protocol that was designed to help you launch the best version of yourSelf by embarking on an inner journey of complete transformation, purification and illumination; 40 days in which to explore the most fulfilling and rewarding Love affair with yourSelf.

This practical guide will show how to enhance your health, clarity, and overall well-being while supporting your natural ability to heal and rejuvenate. You will learn how to cleanse, detoxify, and renew your entire system by using Life-giving foods (numerous wholesome recipes provided), juice cleansing, kundalini yoga as a primary practice, and many applications of Self-care and radical Self-Love in action. During this 40-day journey, you'll get to implement some of the most effective tools I know to help you shift your inner reality, ensuring your consistently in making the best choices for yourSelf in all areas of your Life.

If embarking on this journey calls to you yet you'd like to receive additional support, I invite you to consider my *40 Days to Self-Mastery group program* or working with me one-on-one. This can be a challenging endeavor for many so having someone to hold your hand or being part of a dedicated community can be extremely helpful.

For any additional information regarding private coaching and group programs, please contact Noa at: Noa@Noalakshmi.com or visit: http://www.noalakshmi.com/group-program/

About the author

Noa Lakshmi is an author, Self-Love master coach, lifestyle design specialist, inspirational speaker, intuitive astrologer, yoga teacher, and a guide for many. Her mission is dedicated to the transformational power of Love, especially Self-Love, which is the foundation of her work in the world. For over a decade, Noa has worked with hundreds of individuals, showing them how to cultivate the most loving relationship with themselves and experience profound healing in their body, mind, heart, and soul. The publication of her first book, *Master your Life with Love*, represents a labor of Love designed to activate and unleash one's full human potential.

Noa sees our human experience as a precious gift. From this place of appreciation, Love, and gratitude, her work shares a holistic vision for personal alchemy and cultural transformation. Noa invokes the mantra to "BE the change you wish to see in the world," and she believes we are transforming the world with Love one human at a time.

Noa offers spiritual and holistic guidance, classes, group programs, talks, workshops, and retreats designed to transform lives from the inside out. Her website offers numerous transformational tools such as personal astrology readings, lifestyle design, and her comprehensive *40 Days to Self-Mastery* program for groups and individuals.

By empowering radiance, fulfillment and radical Love, Noa seeks to elevate humanity for a better world. You can learn more at: www.NoaLakshmi.com. If you would like to invite Noa to come speak at your event or to facilitate an event for your local community, please contact her at: Noa@NoaLakshmi.com